THE

DONNA GORRELL

LITTLE, BROWN

KATHRYN MCARTHUR

WORKBOOK

to accompany

THE LITTLE, BROWN HANDBOOK

FOURTH CANADIAN EDITION

PEARSON
Longman

Toronto

ISBN 0-321-15612-9

Executive Acquisitions Editor: Jessica Mosher
Developmental Editor: John Polanszky
Production Editor: Richard di Santo
Production Coordinator: Patricia Ciardullo

1 2 3 4 5   09 08 07 06 05

Printed and bound in Canada.

Contents

Preface

The Little, Brown Workbook is designed as an instructional supplement to the fourth Canadian edition of *The Little, Brown Handbook*. The workbook has been designed to allow instructors to use exercises according to their own teaching styles and the needs of their students. Most of the exercises are adaptable to cooperative group work. The workbook contains supplemental exercises, keyed to the handbook by section and page number so that students can readily access the relevant textual material.

The arrangement of exercises, from whole paper to word, follows the arrangement of the handbook and reflects current rhetorical theory. An introductory section includes exercises to complement the handbook sections on critical thinking, reading, and writing, designed to promote student writing that is proficient and perceptive. Part I focusses on composing processes, featuring exercises on prewriting, thesis development, drafting, revising, paragraph composition, and support for arguments—all of which aim to encourage students in exploring and developing their own ideas. Part II shifts to grammatical sentences, with Chapter 5 containing exercises based on the principles of English grammar and the remaining chapters in the section containing exercises through which students can practise these principles in greater detail. Exercises in Parts III through VII cover sentence problems, ways of constructing effective sentences, and then punctuation, mechanics, and diction. Part VIII provides exercises keyed to a short documented paper.

Wherever possible, exercises have connected discourse. The contexts are mainly those common to academic settings across a variety of disciplines; they avoid concentration on a single field or culture and the overuse of personal experience. A few feature student writing. The exercises also represent a variety of approaches: sentence patterning or combining, controlled composition, original composition, analysis, sentence completion, plus identification and correction wherever necessary.

Answers to the exercises appear in *The Little, Brown Handbook* Instructor's Manual.

Introduction CRITICAL THINKING, READING, AND WRITING

EXERCISE I-1

Thinking and Reading Critically   *I2 (p. 2)*

Working in pairs or small groups, read the following passage, first applying the "Questions for previewing a text," (p. 4) questions, then reading twice, first quickly and then more carefully. In your second reading, mark the words you want to look up in a dictionary, and write notes and questions in the margin that might help if you were to review the passage later. Compare notes with your classmates.

THE PROBLEM OF CHOICE

1   Teachers very often say to me, "Suppose we tell kids that they now have the freedom to choose what they are going to study, and how and when they are going to study it, and they don't choose anything, don't do anything? Then what do we do?" A good many teachers who have tried to open up their classrooms, usually in a junior high school or high school, have said that this has in fact happened.

2   We should try to see this situation through the eyes of the student. For years he has been playing a school game which looks to him about like this. The teacher holds up a hoop and says, "Jump!" He jumps, and if he makes it, he gets a doggy biscuit. Then the teacher raises the hoop a little higher and again says, "Jump!" Another jump, another biscuit. Or, perhaps the student makes a feeble pretense of jumping, saying, "I'm jumping as high as I can, and this is the best I can do." Or, he may lie on the floor

and refuse to jump. But in any case the rules of the game are simple and clear—hoop, jump, biscuit. Now along comes a teacher who says, "We aren't going to play that game anymore; you're going to decide for yourself what you're going to do." What is the student going to think about this? Almost certainly, he is going to think, "They're hiding the hoop! It was bad enough having to jump through it before, but now I have to find it." Then after a while he is likely to think, "On second thought, maybe I don't have to find it. If I just wait long enough, pretty soon that hoop is going to slip out of its hiding place, and then we'll be back to the old game where at least I know the rules and am comfortable."

3   In short, if we make this offer of freedom, choice, self-direction to students who have spent much time in traditional schools, most of them will not trust us or believe us. Given their experience, they are quite right not to. A student in a traditional school learns before long in a hundred different ways that the school is not on his side; that it is working, not for him, but for the community and the state; that it is not interested in him except as he serves its purposes; and that among all the reasons for which the adults in the school do things, his happiness, health, and growth are by far the least important. He has probably also learned that most of the adults in the school do not tell him the truth and indeed are not allowed to—unless they are willing to run the risk of being fired, which most of them are not. They are not independent and responsible persons, free to say what they think, feel, or believe, or to do what seems reasonable and right. They are employees and spokesmen, telling the children whatever the school administration, the school board, the community, or the legislature want the children to be told. Their job is by whatever means they can to "motivate" the students to do whatever the school wants. So, when a school or teacher says that the students don't have to play the old school game anymore, most of them, certainly those who have not been "good students," will not believe it. They would be very foolish if they did. (John Holt, *Freedom and Beyond;* New York: Dell, 1972)

EXERCISE I-2

Summarizing   *I2-d (p. 8)*

The first two paragraphs below are each followed by two summaries. Judge which is the better summary of each paragraph, indicating your choice with a check mark in the space to the left. Summaries should begin with an overall summary statement, have supporting summary statements as necessary, and name the source. For the third paragraph, write a summary on separate paper.

1   During the year 1903 a forty-year-old Detroiter named Henry Ford, having left the employ of the little Detroit Automobile Company with the idea of going into the manufacturing business for himself, designed and built a big and powerful racing car. Why did he do this? He had no great interest in speed; his idea was quite different: he wanted to make a small, light, serviceable vehicle. The reason he built a racing car was that he wanted capital, and to attract capital he had to have a reputation, and in those days when automobiles were thought of as expensive playthings in which the rich could tear noisily along the dusty roads, the way to get a reputation was to build a car that could win races. (Frederick Lewis Allen, *The Big Change*; New York: Harper, 1952, p. 109)

    _____ a. According to Frederick Lewis Allen, Henry Ford built his first automobile, a powerful racing car, in order to gain a reputation with the wealthy as an automobile builder. Once he had attracted capital, he would build the kind of car he wanted to build: a small, practical one (*The Big Change*; New York: Harper, 1952, 109).

    _____ b. In 1903 Henry Ford built a big and powerful racing car. He didn't want to do this; instead he wanted to build a small, sensible car. But in order to get the capital he needed, he first had to have a reputation, so he cleverly built the race car to get the attention of

3

the rich and famous people who drove cars like that and had the money to invest in building them (*The Big Change;* New York: Harper, 1952, 109).

2   The early Sagas spoke, too, of the abundant fruit of excellent quality growing in Greenland, and of the number of cattle that could be pastured there. The Norwegian settlements were located in places that are now at the foot of glaciers. There are Eskimo legends of old houses and churches buried under the ice. The Danish Archaeological Expedition sent out by the National Museum of Copenhagen was never able to find all of the villages mentioned in the old records. But its excavations indicated clearly that the colonists lived in a climate definitely milder than the present one. (Rachel L. Carson, *The Sea Around Us;* New York: Oxford, 1951, p. 180)

_____ a. There is evidence that the climate of Greenland used to be milder than it is today, according to Rachel L. Carson in *The Sea Around Us.* Old records tell of colonists successfully raising fruit and cattle and of villages located where glaciers now stand (New York: Oxford, 1951, 180).

_____ b. In the past, says Rachel L. Carson, abundant fruit and cattle were raised in Greenland. There were settlements in places that now would be at the foot of glaciers. Eskimos tell of houses and churches buried under the ice, and the Danes found in their archaeological expeditions that the climate of Greenland was once milder than it is today (Rachel L. Carson, *The Sea Around Us;* New York: Oxford, 1951, 180).

3   Even where it has long been entrenched, democracy has not proved invariably hospitable to women. Despite the growing number of women entering politics in the U.S., the country is just beginning the journey toward full equality. In the West, women like [former] British Prime Minister Margaret Thatcher and former Norwegian Prime Minister Gro Brundtland have had to struggle against the traditional demands of gender in order to impress their visions on national policies. For decades the Communist states of Europe boasted of political egalitarianism, making a show of filling token government posts with women. But revolution has torn down the facades, revealing just how

cosmetic was the "power" shared by the East's women. Now the emergence of a new order is challenging women to show themselves both willing and able to take on real responsibilities. (Johanna McGeary, "Challenge in the East," *Time* Special Issue Fall 1990: 30)

EXERCISE I-3

Forming your Critical Response—Analysing, Interpreting, Synthesizing, Evaluating   *I2-e (p. 10)*

Working in pairs, individually, or in groups, read the following para-graphs critically. After your initial reading, work with your partners in analysing the paragraphs for unstated meanings, making notes for a possible critical essay. Apply the "Guidelines for evaluation," (p. 13) to evaluate the paragraphs from the experience and knowledge you and your partners share.

1   Appearance is a symbolic means of self-expression. In the United States clothes are practically a language because there is so much emphasis on how people look, what they buy, and how they package themselves. Over the past decade there have been several revolutions in clothes styles, hair styles, and general personal appearance: boots, levi's, sandals, and military uniforms have replaced pennyloafers, polo shirts, and pegged pants; Madison Avenue types and orthodontists sprout mustaches and sideburns; the suit-and-tie business uniform is embellished with (if not dis-carded for) wide wild ties, colored shirts, cut and flared jackets, and turtlenecks; women wear pants, their skirt hems are at the extremes of floor and crotch, and the underwear industry may go out of business. Restaurants have nearly given up excluding women in pants and men without jackets or ties. Employers, with rare exceptions, no longer try to control the hair growth—facial or cranial—of their employees. (Jean Strouse, *Up Against the Law: The Legal Rights of People Under 21;* New York: Signet, 1970)

2   When in the course of human events it becomes necessary for one people to dissolve the political bands which have connected them with another and to assume among the powers of the earth the separate and equal station to which the law of nature and of nature's God entitle them, a decent respect to the opinions of mankind requires that they should declare the causes which impel them to the separation. We hold these truths to be self-evident,

that all men are created equal, that they are endowed by their Creator with certain unalienable rights, that among these are life, liberty, and the pursuit of happiness. That to secure these rights, governments are instituted among men, deriving their just powers from the consent of the governed. That whenever any form of government becomes destructive of these ends, it is the right of the people to alter or to abolish it, and to institute new government, laying its foundation on such principles and organizing its powers in such form as to them shall seem most likely to effect their safety and happiness. (Thomas Jefferson, *The Declaration of Independence*, 1776)

3   The maids and doormen, factory workers and janitors who were able to leave their ghetto homes and rub against the cold-shouldered white world told themselves that things were not as bad as they seemed. They smiled a dishonest acceptance at their mean servitude and on Saturday night bought the most expensive liquor to drown their lie. Others, locked in the unending maze of having to laugh without humor and scratch without agitation, foisted their hopes on the Lord. They shouted loudly on Sunday morning at His goodness and spent the afternoon preparing the starched uniforms to meet a boss's unrelenting examination. The timorous and frightened held tightly to their palliatives. I was neither timid nor afraid. (Maya Angelou, *Gather Together in My Name;* New York: Bantam, 1974)

EXERCISE I-4

Forming your Critical Response—Analysing, Interpreting, Synthesizing, Evaluating   *I2-e (p. 10)*

Write a short essay based on your critical reading of one of the paragraphs in Exercise I-3. Follow the guidelines on page 16–17 (LBH).

Part I   THE WHOLE PAPER AND PARAGRAPHS

Chapter 1   Developing an Essay

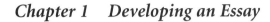

EXERCISE 1-1

Discovering and Limiting a Subject   *1b (p. 23)*

Use these questions for discovering a subject for an essay when you are not assigned one. Answer the questions as completely as you can, using separate paper.

I. Entertainment.

   A. What books, stories, or magazine articles have I read recently?

   B. What programs have I seen recently on television that interested me?

   C. What movies have I seen recently and liked?

II. Choose one of your answers in A, B, or C of Part 1.

   A. What made that story, program, or movie good?

   B. Why do I remember that story, program, or movie?

   C. What scenes or parts did I like best? Why?

   D. Which character seemed most realistic to me? Why?

III. Issues.

   A. What local or national issues interest me?

   B. Why am I interested in any one of those issues?

   C. What features of that issue are most controversial?

D. What is the most challenging idea I've heard in the past two weeks?

E. Why does that idea seem challenging to me?

F. What interesting discussions have I had lately?

IV. Goals.

A. What is the most important goal in my life?

B. What am I willing to do to achieve that goal?

C. How did I decide that it is a worthy goal for me?

V. Persons.

A. What person do I most admire?

B. What do I admire about that person?

EXERCISE 1-2

Analysing Tone   *1d (p. 28)*

Read the following passages and, with a classmate, discuss (1) their tone and the features of the writing that contribute toward the tone, and (2) what assumptions the writer has made about the audience (see Questions about audience on pages 28–29).

1   [Nelson] Mandela may lack the rousing, bred-in-the-pulpit style of black orators like [Martin Luther] King or Jesse Jackson. His soft-spoken manner and unflappable dignity bespeak his background as a lawyer, a single-minded political organizer and a longtime prisoner still blinking a bit in the spotlight. But Mandela's magnetism is palpable, the consequence of his endurance and determination in the fight against South Africa's white-minority government. He fires the pride of African Americans and touches a deep desire in the psyche of Americans both black and white for a leader who might rekindle the biracial coalition that destroyed their country's own version of apartheid a generation ago, then fell apart during the long, hot summers of the '60s (*Time* 2 July 1990:15-16).

2   She wanted a house with air conditioning. I wanted a house with more than one bathroom. The house we bought has an air conditioner big enough to cool Saudi Arabia. And one bathroom. She wanted a house with hardwood floors. I wanted one with a Jacuzzi big enough for two persons. The house we bought has floors hard enough to shatter a woodpecker's beak. And a bathtub big enough to hold two minor body parts. She wanted an older house with "character." I wanted a house in which the builders still were pounding the nails three weeks after we moved in. The house we bought has bullet holes in it from the Civil War. (*St. Cloud Times* 13 Oct. 1990: 5)

3   The world's dolphins are being decimated through a deadly combination of commercial greed and plain human carelessness. In the next five years, international tuna fishing fleets in the eastern tropical Pacific will legally slaughter more than three hundred seventy-five thousand of these intelligent animals unless you and I act now to save them. Greenpeace urgently needs you to join our international campaign to stop this tragedy. It's going to take all the ingenuity, energy, and resources we can muster before victory is won. And we must act quickly. (Greenpeace letter, no date)

EXERCISE 1-3

Developing a Subject Through Freewriting   *1e-3 (p. 34)*

Choose *one* of the broad subjects in Exercise 1-1, for example "a person I admire" or "my goals in life," and, on separate paper, write about it for fifteen minutes without stopping, without correcting spelling or other errors, and without concern for organization or thesis. Just write. Fill both sides of the page. When you have finished, read what you have written to see whether a central idea is emerging.

EXERCISE 1-4

Generating Ideas   *1e (p. 32)*

Choose a specific topic, perhaps one of those you identified in Exercise 1-1 or 1-3. On separate paper, develop ideas for a brief essay, using two of the methods discussed on pages 33-38, such as freewriting, list making, clustering, reading, asking the journalist's questions, or asking questions based on patterns of development. For example, if you'd like to write on a personal goal, you might start by freewriting and then ask questions based on patterns of development.

Name _____ Date _____

EXERCISE 1-5

Revising the Thesis Sentence   1f-2 (p. 43)

Rewrite the following thesis sentences to make them specific, limited, and unified.

> *Example:* Members of Parliament do not communicate enough with their constituents.
>
> *Members of Parliament should improve communication with voters by regularly scheduling local meetings and by mailing newsletters before and after parliamentary sessions.*

1. Many people believe that teachers have no right to strike.

2. Religious cults serve a valid purpose.

3. The government owes a university education to every citizen who wants one.

4. The hunting of wild animals, as long as they are not in danger of extinction, can actually help nature.

5. Travel to foreign countries is educational.

6. Silence is often the best response to anger.

EXERCISE 1-6

Developing the Thesis Sentence   *1f-2 (p. 43)*

Select one of the subjects you discovered in Exercise 1-1 or 1-3, perhaps the same one you worked with in Exercise 1-4, or use an assigned
subject. After answering the following questions about that subject,
write a thesis sentence at the bottom of the page.

  1. How am I related to the subject (expert, angry citizen, informed
     student, mature youth, and so on)?

  2. What interests me about the subject?

  3. Why do I want to write about the subject?

  4. How do I want my audience to react to my essay?

  5. Who might want to read about my subject?

  6. Why do I want to read about it? (Is the answer different from your
     answer to 5?)

  7. What do I want to say? (*Not* "What do I want to write about?"—
     your subject—but "What do I want to *say* about it?"—your asser-
     tion.)

Thesis sentence:

EXERCISE 1-7

The Formal Outline   *1g (p. 46)*

On separate paper, rewrite the following informal outline (which has
no indications of subordinate ideas) into a formal outline, using as
many subdivisions as necessary to put parallel ideas into parallel for-
mat. Refer to the outline on page 50 as a guide, remembering that you
will have different divisions and subdivisions.

Thesis sentence

Because flying terrifies me, I have developed several techniques to
help me cope with that fear both before and during a flight.

Informal outline

1. Introduction
2. Narrative of last plane trip
3. Recounting fear of flying
4. Statement of thesis
5. Relaxation methods before a flight
6. Trying to sleep the night before
7. Reading an architecture book before sleeping
8. Contemplating pictures before sleeping
9. Riding to the airport
10. Talking to the cab driver
11. Looking out the cab window
12. Reading in the airport lounge
13. Relaxation methods during a flight
14. Taking a seat
15. Choosing a seat location
16. Choosing a travel companion
17. Eating
18. Reading
19. Listening to music
20. Staying in my seat
21. Refraining from looking out the window
22. Conclusion
23. Restatement of thesis

EXERCISE 1-8

Outlining an Essay   *1g (p. 46)*

One use for outlines is to check the organization of a piece you've already written. Read the following essay and, on separate paper, write an outline of it, following the guidelines for formal outlines on page 50. Start by stating the thesis.

HOME AWAY FROM HOME

The term "home" can be defined in many ways: house, family, neighbourhood, town, and so on. When you ask people to define home, they will most likely describe a place where they enjoyed themselves more than anywhere else. I define home as a place where a person lives freely and confidently and finds happiness. My perception of home has changed over the years as I have changed.

I lived the first thirteen years of my life in a medium-sized, ordinary, and some might say boring city called Normal. The name says it all. Life there revolves around family, school, church, athletics, and designer clothes—a preppy's paradise. While I lived there, I thought of home as my family and my neighbourhood. I rarely went out of my neighbourhood; when I did, I usually went with a friend who lived in my neighbourhood. Quite often we would even bump into someone from our neighbourhood. In Normal, all of my friends were nearby. I spent all my time playing tag, whiffleball, hide-and-seek, and other childhood favourites with the neighbourhood kids. I was content with life and loved my friends; I had no room in my life for change.

The main cause of my changed perception of home was my family's move to Toronto. I was devastated when I heard the news and wondered how I would live through it. During my first year in Toronto I still called Normal home. My best friends and memories were there and I wasn't. All I wanted to do was go home. Only then I considered Normal my home, not just my quaint little neighbourhood in Normal. I became dejected in Toronto and didn't look forward to my life in the unfamiliar city. Eventually I made good friends who showed me the ways of the big city, and I came to like Toronto.

Once I enjoyed life in Toronto, I considered it my home. I adjusted to the major change in my life and made the best of it. The best four years of my life have been while I have lived in Toronto. I have found Toronto to be a place where I can be myself and still be appreciated and accepted, unlike in Normal. Right now I define home as a place where people can be themselves and enjoy life.

At this time, I really love living in Toronto and feel I will always consider it my home, even when I move away. Of course, as I change so will my views of other things, including home. I believe that wherever I truly enjoy being who I am and doing what I do, I will call home.

—STUDENT ESSAY

EXERCISE 1-9

Writing an Outline for an Essay   *1g (p. 46)*

Prepare an outline for an essay, using the ideas you generated in Exercise 1-4. First, repeat the thesis sentence composed in Exercise 1-6. Then outline the ideas, using the form (informal or formal) specified by your instructor. Be sure the outline is unified (all its parts relate to one another and to the thesis) and coherent (the relations among ideas are logical and clear). Your instructor may ask you and a classmate to exchange outlines and check unity and coherence.

Chapter 2   Drafting and Revising the Essay

EXERCISE 2-1

Revising the First Draft   *2a (p. 57)*

Read this rough draft of a student essay, applying the checklist for revision on page 63. Write a response to a classmate, using the guidelines for criticizing others' work on pages 72–73. At this point you may not want to call attention to all the errors. Write your response at the end of the exercise, and make notes in the draft wherever you want to call something to the writer's attention.

SOCIOLOGY—MORE THAN A CLASS

1   Sociology is a class we take at school. Because it is a required course or we need the extra credits. It is taken so we may become more knowledgeable and intelligent. This in turn helps us to obtain a good passing grade. Therefore, we are able to graduate, from there we go out into society and get a job. When we hear the term sociology we feel it is only a course taken at school, it could not have any essential meaning or value to us. It is often confused with anthropology and psychology. Sociology is not only a class, its a vital force of life.

2   At some point in life we all wonder how a particular event may effect our lives. There is a feeling of bewilderment. If we are ignorant on a certain issue, it's value may be overlooked. We will try to rationalize to ourselves and to others how this is of no significance to us. We are effected by sociology everyday of our lives.

19

3   Society is made up of people who share the same enviorment. The enviorment in which we live effects the way we act and react to other people and situations. For example, the way we speak to our children may vary, depending on where we are and if their's anyone else nearby. In turn our behaviour is being affected, or controlled, by the enviorment. Sociology is what people are doing and how they interact with others. It can also be defined more accuratly as the study of social life, and the social consequences of human behaviour.

4   Some sociologists believe that people interact with others on three levels; individual interaction, group interaction, and structural interaction. Individual interaction is how we deal with people on a one to one basis. Group interaction is how three or more people interact as a whole. Structural interaction is how people react to a situation that is controlled by the enviorment.

5   Sociology helps us to better understand ourselves, other people, and the framework of society. If we, the society as a whole, could gain a new perspective on sociology, and the affects it has on humanity, we could understand how and why things happen in this world. If we acknowledge the misconception that sociology is just a class, we are denying ourselves the opportunity to become more enlightened, and perceptive to the ways of life.

EXERCISE 2-2

Using the Correction Symbols   *2b (p. 58)*

The errors in the following paragraphs are marked with the correction symbols shown inside the back cover of the text. On separate paper, revise the paragraphs according to the markings.

TOUGH TRIP

no cap 26f — In Western Canada, travelling in the winter
sp 34 — can be hazerdous and frusturating. The roads
and whether conditions may be perfectly clear
when the travller leaves home but after a few *p∧ 21a*
days of visiting relatives or taking care of
business, the conditions may have changed *agr 8a*
cs // — drastically. My family and I has experienced
such problems often, possibly the worse *ad 9e*
sp 34 — occurance was last year after Christmas when *cap 26 / sp 34*
we were returning from visiting our
grandparents in Calgary.

The trip was particularly bad for the last
one hundred and fifty kilometres or so between
the Alberta border and Swift Current. While
the highway going through Alberta was wet and
p 22e — messy; the road as we entered Saskatchewan
became snow-covered and slick. And the farther
no cap 26f — we drove into our home Province, the worse the
roads become. From the 100-kilometre-per-hour
sp 34 — speed that was common on the Trans-Canada,
the traffic slowed to 80, then to 60.

Continuing to drop to about 40 and 30. Even at *frag 10* 30 kilometres per hour, stoping was impossible, we just drove along slowly, hoping *sp 34* that there would be no need to stop. All along *cs //* the way the shoulders were punctuated by cars and trucks that had tried to do something different. Then to plod along at a regular *sp 34* *frag 10* though agonizingly slow rate of speed. The closer we got to home, the worse it became. *ref 8b*

sp 34 The absolute worst occured after we entered the city. Choosing to drive through downtown, thinking that those streets would most likely *frag 10* be cleared (and going that way was the most direct route to our house). We drove into a huge traffic snarl made up of cars, trucks, and buses stuck in and grinding away at the entire twenty centimetres of damp, slushy, *p 21f* slippery no-longer-white stuff occupying the major intersections. The ploughing crews were waiting for people to go home so they can *7f* *agr 8a* clear the streets, but the only way people could go home were to push their cars around the stuck ones and out of the slush.

After we got home and turned on the radio, we heard what we already knew: the storm had dumped twenty centimetres of snow in just a few hours, whereas areas to the south had *sp 34* recieved a mere five or six centimetres, and farther to the south their was rain. After *sp 34* shovelling out the driveway() and puting away the car, we were glad to be home. *p 21f*

Chapter 3   *Writing and Revising Paragraphs*

EXERCISE 3-1

Identifying Irrelevant Details   *3a (p. 78)*

The topic sentence is italicized in each of the two paragraphs below. Each paragraph contains sentences that are not directly related to the central idea. Identify these irrelevant sentences by drawing a line through them. Then reread each paragraph to check for improved unity; if all sentences still are not supporting the topic sentence, make further deletions until you are satisfied that all sentences support the central idea.

1   We tend to view mosquitoes as insects with identical traits and with the primary goal of sucking human juices. *But there is quite a bit of variety among mosquitoes, as their biting behaviour illustrates.* The female mosquito tries to lay her eggs where there is water or is certain to be water. It was once thought that only female mosquitoes bite, but in at least one group males also feed and both sexes feed only on flowers, not on animals. In another group, females feed by sticking a tube into an ant's mouth for a secretion the ant has collected from aphids. Mating habits also vary widely among mosquitoes. Feeding on animals, including humans, may occur after mating, when the female needs food for her eggs. But some groups of mosquitoes never do bother humans at all, getting their food instead exclusively from birds or other animals.

2   *English pubs illustrate English character.* Every neighbourhood has a pub that serves as its social centre. The local residents congregate in the sedate and home-like atmosphere of soft talk, warm lights, and comfortable furniture, drinking mostly pints of beer or ale. In Canada, by contrast, bars are loud with music, dark and shadowy, and furnished with hard chairs and benches. One can go to a Canadian bar and expect to remain anonymous, hidden from

view and free of the annoyances of human interaction. The pubs close their doors promptly at ten on weeknights and eleven on weekends, at which point everyone returns home. Thus the pubs almost dictate English leisure life, whose principle seems to be pleasure under control.

EXERCISE 3-2

Identifying the Topic Sentence   *3a (p. 78)*

The topic sentences in the following paragraphs occur at different points—at the beginning, at the end, or somewhere in between. Working alone or with classmates, identify the topic sentence in each paragraph and underline it.

1   Diamonds are the hardest naturally occurring substance known. They are so hard that they can cut and grind very hard metal. To accomplish such tasks, they are sometimes set in the ends of drills and other tools. At other times they are crushed into dust and baked into industrial tools. Because of their extreme hardness and indestructibility, they are also used as needles in all record players.

2   Diamonds can be broken with a severe blow. If they are put in acid, they will dissolve. If they are heated in the presence of oxygen, they will burn and form carbon dioxide. If they are heated without oxygen, they turn to graphite, a very soft mineral. So, even though diamonds are the hardest natural substance known, there are ways of destroying them.

3   Diamonds are made up of many sides, or facets, each of which must be the right size and shape and placed at exactly the right angle. Each must be polished. Because of these facets, diamonds are sparklingly brilliant. Each facet reflects light, bends rays of light, and breaks light up into the colours of the rainbow.

4   There are only four major sources of diamonds: Africa, India, Siberia, and South America. Africa is by far the largest producer, mining about 80 percent of the world's supply. Most of the remainder come from Siberia, which produces about 16 percent. India, although once an important source, mines very few of the gems today, and South America also accounts for a small number.

Name _____ Date _____

EXERCISE 3-3

Organizing Paragraphs: Spatial Order   *3b (p. 86)*

Below is the topic sentence for a paragraph organized spatially. Following the topic sentence, in random order, are the sentences that develop it. Reorder the sentences into spatial order by numbering them in the spaces to their left. The topic sentence is numbered already. Your instructor may ask you to do this part of the exercise in pairs or groups. After you have correctly numbered the sentences, write the paragraph on separate paper, putting the sentences in logical order.

Spatial order:

_*1*_   **Topic sentence:** From head to foot he was clearly dressed for a Winnipeg winter.

_____   His chin was somewhere beneath a plaid scarf that encircled his neck and lower face.

_____   His legs were protected from the elements too, encased in lined and quilted pants of a vague greenish colour.

_____   The coat was of the type that has an industrial-strength zipper hidden beneath a fly that fastens down with toggles.

_____   His thick coat sleeves ended in sheepskin mittens, the soft leather exposed to the outside, the furry interior wrapping and warming his hands.

_____   A fur-lined parka covered his head and enveloped his wind-burned face, seeming to put his eyes at the end of a dark tunnel.

_____   Under the scarf his bulky coat—quilted, down-filled, an indistinct greyish brown—attached to the base of the parka.

_____   Finally, on his feet were heavy leather boots, laced up above his ankles, topped with the red-striped cuffs of his wool socks.

_____   One of the toggle buttons was missing, leaving a creased gap that revealed the heavy zipper underneath.

EXERCISE 3-4

Organizing Paragraphs: Chronological Order   *3b (p. 86)*

Below is the topic sentence for a paragraph organized chronologically. Following the topic sentence, in random order, are the sentences that develop it. Reorder the sentences into chronological order by numbering them in the spaces to their left. The topic sentence is numbered already. Your instructor may ask you to do this part of the exercise in pairs or groups. After you have correctly numbered the sentences, write the paragraph on separate paper, putting the sentences in logical order.

Chronological order:

_____1_____ **Topic sentence:** This is how I make my high-caloric, high-cholesterol, irresistible caramels.

_____ Into a heavy saucepan I put the sugar, the corn syrup, one cup of the cream, and a dash of salt.

_____ Then I remove it from the pan and, with a large, sharp knife, cut it into those melt-in-your-mouth, irresistible little cubes.

_____ Once it has begun to boil, I attach a candy thermometer to the side of the pan, turn the heat down, and let the mixture cook to the soft-ball stage, about 235 degrees.

_____ When the soft-ball stage has been reached for the second time, I add the stick of butter and continue cooking until the mixture reaches almost 246 degrees.

_____ First, I get out all the ingredients: a pint of cream, a stick of butter, two cups of sugar, one cup of white corn syrup, a bit of salt, and the bottle of vanilla.

_____ By now it has become a medium brown.

_____ At each soft-ball stage the mixture is a light brown colour.

_____ I set the saucepan on medium heat and stir the mixture while it comes to a boil.

_____ I remove the saucepan from the heat, take out the thermometer, and stir in one teaspoon of vanilla.

_____ Then I add the remaining cream, bringing the mixture to a boil again, and I cook it again to the soft-ball stage.

_____ Quickly I pour the hot caramel mixture into a nine-by-nine-inch buttered pan and let it set to cool and become firm.

EXERCISE 3-5

Organizing Paragraphs: Specific to General   *3b (p. 87)*

Below is the topic sentence for a paragraph organized from specific to general. Following the topic sentence, in random order, are the sentences that develop it. Reorder the sentences into specific-to-general order by numbering them in the spaces to their left. The topic sentence is numbered already. Your instructor may ask you to do this part of the exercise in pairs or groups. After you have correctly numbered the sentences, write the paragraph on separate paper, putting the sentences in logical order.

Specific to general:

_7_   **Topic sentence:** Golden retriever, both as pets and as working dogs, have become one of the most popular breeds in North America.

_____   Similarly, observing a working golden retriever confidently and safely guide a visually impaired teenager through a crowd and across a street inspires respect.

_____   A golden retriever will bound up to a toddler and mother, eager to play, and then, at a single gentle command, sit quietly so as not to frighten either and let them make the first move in friendship.

_____   Seeing a golden retriever with its characteristic "smile" and happily waving tail gently nuzzle the face of a small child in a playground warms the heart of any onlooker.

_____   This willing obedience, sense of the behaviour requirements of a given situation and a native intelligence combine to make this breed of dog the most often successful as a guide dog for the visually impaired.

_____   Goldens are "people" dogs, friendly, gentle, loyal and eager, they actually require and seek out human direction and companionship.

_____   They also love to learn and excel at specific "jobs" and in obedience and field trials.

29

Name _____ Date _____

EXERCISE 3-6

Organizing Paragraphs: Climactic Order   *3b (p. 88)*

Below is the topic sentence for a paragraph organized in climactic order. Following it, in random order, are the sentences that develop it. Reorder the sentences into dramatic order by numbering them in the spaces to their left. The topic sentence is numbered already. Your instructor may ask you to do this part of the exercise in pairs or groups. After you have correctly numbered the sentences, write the paragraph, putting the sentences in logical order.

Dramatic order:

___*1*___ **Topic sentence:** I could tell as I saw Dusty step onto the stack of papers that something terrible was about to happen.

_____ As the books quivered under her, the flowerpot with three little seedlings, sitting atop the books to catch the afternoon sun, lost its footing.

_____ First the papers started to slide, exposing beneath them the magazines and computer disks.

_____ When they crashed, it was in a pile of dirt—all except Dusty (she was nowhere to be found) and the seedlings (they were no more).

_____ They too began to move.

_____ The entire stack was immediately in motion, and Dusty began shifting her weight to the books.

_____ When she stepped up to the pile of books, leaving her back paws still on the papers, it began.

_____ Suddenly everything was in the air: papers, magazines, computer disks, books, flowerpot, and cat.

EXERCISE 3-7

Being Consistent   *3b-5 (p. 90)*

The following paragraphs contain inappropriate shifts in person, number, and tense. Underline each shift and write the correct word in the space above it.

1   One year I went to Point Pelée, Ontario, from my home in Dauphin, Manitoba, to see the great blue heron during its fall migration. As we travelled between Dauphin and the conservation area, you could see several flocks of heron flying south—five or six hundred at a time. They probably have spent the late fall months in various parts of southern Ontario and are not ready to move on until their food supply there was exhausted.

2   At Burger King the menu is displayed on the wall above the area where the food is cooked and where you placed and pay for your order. The selections included hamburgers, specialty sandwiches, side orders, beverages and desserts. The price of the special "deals" ranged from three to six dollars. After ordering and paying, the customers wait in line for their food to be cooked, as you would in a cafeteria. After a few minutes, you are handed your food on trays and we serve as our own wait staff. The customer either sat down alone or with other customers at small plastic tables with attached chairs familiar from other fast-food restaurants

3   Plants serve two purposes in an aquarium. First, a plant is ornamental, making an otherwise plain aquarium attractive. But more important, plants help to maintain healthy conditions in aquariums. A plant does this by removing nitrogenous wastes from the water and from the aquarium gravel. Plants do not, as commonly believed, add a significant amount of oxygen to the water. While they do produce oxygen during the day, at night they would take oxygen out of the water.

Name _____ Date _____

EXERCISE 3-8

Arranging and Linking Sentences   *3b-6, 7 (p. 91–95)*

The following list provides all the details for a unified and coherent paragraph about a volcanic eruption on the island of Krakatoa. Through combining sentences, rearranging details, and using some of the coherence devices discussed in this chapter, you can write a paragraph that describes the explosion and its effects. Begin with the topic sentence and combine it with the clarifying sentence, reducing unnecessary words by using only the *when* clause of the clarifying sentence. Select details in chronological order, and finish with the concluding sentence. Use parallelism, repetition of key words, pronouns with clear references, and transitional expressions.

TOPIC SENTENCE
The greatest volcanic eruption of modern times occurred on August 27, 1883.

CLARIFYING SENTENCE
The great eruption occurred when the island of Krakatoa, in what is now Indonesia, blew up.

CONCLUDING SENTENCE
In the aftermath nearly forty thousand people were discovered to have died.

1. The mountains exploded.
2. The island sank into the ocean.
3. At first the island's mountains spewed rocks and ash into the air for a day, blackening the sky.
4. The earth calmed down again.
5. The explosion roared.
6. The collapse of the island caused gigantic tidal waves.
7. Almost nothing remained of the island when things were calm again.
8. The sound could be heard three thousand miles away.
9. The tidal waves swallowed up coastal cities and inland towns.
10. The explosion created winds that circled the earth several times.
11. The waves appeared finally as unusually large waves on the English coast, half a world away.

EXERCISE 3-9

Identifying Parallelism, Repetition, Pronouns, and Transitional Expressions   *3b-7 (p. 92)*

Read the following paragraph, looking for the ways in which parallelism, repetition, pronouns, and transitional expressions link sentences. Then answer the questions that follow. After completing the exercise, apply the same type of analysis to one of your paragraphs.

> The most notable house in Plainville has always been a
> large and distinguished Victorian on Grant Avenue. The
> house was built in the 1890s by a wealthy industrialist who
> claimed to see great promise in the backwater town. The
> promise was never fulfilled, however, and the town settled
> instead into permanent shabbiness and obscurity. Despite his
> disappointments, the industrialist and three succeeding generations of his family stayed on in the mansion, preserving it
> for themselves and thus for their neighbours. Standing a full
> storey above anything else in Plainville, the house remained a
> source of pleasure and pride for the community. Painted
> royal blue with red trim, it provided a bright island in an otherwise colourless setting. Even when the house was finally
> abandoned in the 1970s, it still recalled Plainville's optimistic
> past. Last week that past was demolished along with the old
> house. Now all that remains in Plainville is the drab present.

(line numbers: 1 2 3 4 5 6 7 8 9)

1. List at least five transitional expressions in the paragraph.

   a. _____

   b. _____

   c. _____

   d. _____

   e. _____

2. Two key words in the first sentence are *house* and *Plainville*. List five repetitions or restatements (pronouns and synonyms) of each one in the order in which they appear in the paragraph.

a. Key word: *house*

Repetitions or restatements: _____;

_____; _____; _____;

_____

b. Key word: *Plainville*

Repetitions or restatements: _____;

_____; _____; _____;

_____; _____; _____

3. The paragraph also contains three other words that are repeated in at least two sentences each. List them.

a. _____ b. _____ c. _____

4. Pronouns substitute for three different nouns in the paragraph. Identify each noun and list the pronoun or pronouns substituting for each one.

a. Noun: _____ Pronoun(s): _____

b. Noun: _____ Pronoun(s): _____

c. Noun: _____ Pronoun(s): _____

5. Two descriptive sentences in the paragraph are closely linked by parallelism. Identify the sentences by number.

a. _____ b. _____

EXERCISE 3-10

Using Paragraph Patterns of Development   *3c (p. 95)*

Drawing on the topics suggested below or on topics of your own, and selecting appropriate readers and purposes, develop a paragraph for each pattern of development. Underline your topic sentence.

1. Topics for **narration:** an accident; a frightening experience; your first morning at college.

2. Topics for **description:** a new friend; a recent purchase; the car you want to drive.

3. Topics for **examples:** how television commercials mislead; the ideal shopping centre; what stage fright is like.

4. Topics for **reasons:** why not to buy sweetened cereals; why to read newspapers; why a particular person makes you feel important.

5. Topics for **definition:** loyalty; authority; education; worrying.

6. Topics for **division:** (parts of) a football team; a concert; a newspaper.

7. Topics for **classification:** (types of) diets; students; comic strips; music.

8. Topics for **comparison, contrast, or both:** two persons' ways of laughing; news reports on radio and television; two diet plans.

9. Topics for **analogy:** In some ways a classroom is like a church or a synagogue; writing is like a bus trip; jealousy is like hunger.

10. Topics for **cause-and-effect analysis:** the physical effects of anger; the effects of a rainstorm (or some other natural event); why you're taking a particular class; why you never (or always) travel by bus or train.

11. Topics for **process analysis:** how to argue with a traffic officer; how dogs (or cats or some other pet) let you know it's time for them to eat; how to clean a room.

EXERCISE 3-11

Opening and Closing an Essay   *3d (p. 109)*

Here are the introductions and conclusions for three essays. On the lines below each introduction, tell whether the paragraph uses statement of subject, background information, anecdote, opinion, historical fact or event, question, or something else. On the lines below each conclusion, tell whether the paragraph uses summary, question, facts, quotation, suggestion of a course of action, or something else. For both introductions and conclusions, name as many devices as you find.

1. *Introduction:* Men die about seven years sooner than women. Whether they want to admit it or not, the males of the species are more fragile than the females. Men have a biologic makeup that causes them to over-react to stress, thus putting undue strain on the cardiovascular system and causing it to wear out sooner. But there is good news: men can improve their chances for a longer life by making a few changes in their lifestyle.

   _____

   _____

   _____

   Conclusion: As a result of making these few changes—increasing exercise, stopping smoking, adopting a low-cholesterol diet, and possibly changing professions—most men can look forward to enjoying old age with their sweethearts. Now isn't that worth a few lifestyle changes?

   _____

   _____

   _____

2. *Introduction:* In 1956 a group of Africanized killer bees escaped from a researcher in Brazil and have been spreading throughout the North and South American continents ever since. They have

been moving northward steadily, and perhaps already have reached the southern United States. Unlike their tamer cousins—the honeybees, well known in this hemisphere—the killer bees are a particularly vicious, aggressive variety, attacking with little provocation.

_____

_____

_____

Conclusion: As these documented instances illustrate, the immigration of the bees is a formidable problem, one for which scientists still have no solution. Let's hope that in the near future researchers will find ways to stop the killer bees or alter their behaviour.

_____

_____

_____

3. *Introduction:* An increasing problem on Canada's waterways is boaters operating their vessels while under the influence of alcohol or drugs. While there are many reasons to account for boating accidents, at least half of all accidents on the water can be blamed on alcohol and drugs. Fortunately, most provinces and finally the federal government have laws prohibiting boaters from operating their vessels while under the influence of intoxicants.

_____

_____

_____

Conclusion: With these new laws on the books, perhaps we will see a decrease in the senseless accidents that have frequented our waterways. As one boater has said, "I'm in favour of anything that cleans up the sport." Let's clean it up.

_____

_____

_____

Name _____ Date _____

EXERCISE 3-12

Analysing an Essay's Coherence   *3e (p. 115)*

Working individually or in a group, analyse the following essay for coherence both within and between paragraphs. Circle all repetitions of key words (and related synonyms and pronouns), drawing lines to connect them. Underline all instances of parallelism, connecting them with dotted lines. Enclose transitional expressions in boxes.

ASSISTANCE

Jane Hill (Student Writer)

1   Most people have a vague idea of what it means to provide assistance to others. In the grocery store, assistance means finding a requested food item or carrying out heavy sacks for an elderly customer; for a parent, assistance means tying shoes or buttoning shirts. In the office, assistance may be providing technical expertise in a specific area. In school, assistance may take the form of tutoring at the writing or reading centre. The word *assistance* implies helpfulness and aid. In the world of human services, however, assistance means welfare.

2   For a single parent, assistance provides financial support based on the loss of the absent parent's income. This assistance, or welfare, is provided in the form of cash to meet the maintenance needs of the family. The dollar amounts increase proportionately according to household size. They are set by the government, and, in this province, have not increased in several years. Can a young mother of two really be expected to shelter, clothe, and feed her family on the same welfare amount paid out several years ago? Is this assistance?

3   Additional assistance in this country has been traditionally provided by the universal health-care system, but in the last decade this system has been gradually eroded by the increase in premiums and user fees. Families who were found to be eligible for cash benefits were also traditionally assisted with drug- and other health-care costs. However, not all medical 'extras' like user fees and prescription costs are now covered. What is this assistance for medical care providing if so many other costs are no longer covered?

4   The problem of medical assistance is intensified for the elderly and disabled, who are allowed to keep only a limited amount of their income and still remain eligible for full prescription and other medical costs. Should an elderly widow be forced to spend most of her meagre income on medicine for the ravages of ageing? What type of standard of living have we given to society's parents and grandparents in return for their years of contributions to its well-being?

5   Some people see problems in making assistance readily available to the poor. In this country, a single adult who is destitute may qualify for cash assistance. Because the amount of this assistance is not equal in all provinces, it has been cited as a contributing factor in the increased transient and migrant population in the summer months. I have seen little objective evidence to support this contention, however. I am at a loss to understand why a person would relocate from a distance so great as that between provinces for a meagre increase per month. Further, I have some difficulty understanding how a person even survives on these small amounts of money.

6   For many in our society today, assistance, or welfare, has a negative connotation. The word *assistance* in general describes positive events and helpful actions. Has its definition changed, or, perhaps, is our society giving mere lip service to its intended application in the case of welfare assistance? Has the assistance provided by the welfare system really carried out the groceries for its recipients in the same spirit as the grocery store clerk? If not, then it's clear that the word *assistance* in this case is a misnomer.

Name _____ Date _____

Chapter 4 Reading and Writing Arguments

EXERCISE 4-1

Testing Assertions   *4a-1 (p. 122)*

Alone or with classmates, read the following assertions and identify them as (1) fact, (2) opinion, (3) belief, or (4) prejudice.

> *Example:*   _*1*_ John Ritter, father on TV's *Eight Simple Rules,* died
> September 11, 2003.

_____ 1. Pierre Trudeau was the most honourable Prime Minister Canada has ever had.

_____ 2. Pierre Trudeau invoked the War Measures Act in October 1970 after the kidnapping of British diplomat James Cross.

_____ 3. The Babylon built by Nebuchadnezzar II was a magnificent city.

_____ 4. Captain William Kidd was hanged in 1701 for piracy.

_____ 5. Indira Gandhi, the prime minister of India, was assassinated on October 31, 1984, in New Delhi.

_____ 6. Truth comes out of heated discussion.

_____ 7. Every university student should take at least one history course in order to have a better understanding of world events.

_____ 8. Pro-abortionists have little regard for human life.

_____ 9. These economic policies are designed to encourage local entrepreneurial activity.

_____ 10. Working mothers neglect their children.

_____ 11. People with AIDS ask only what other people ask—not to be discriminated against.

_____ 12. Parents and guardians who abuse their children should be shot.

_____ 13. Animal experimentation can be beneficial to people.

_____ 14. In 1989, a Texas court sentenced Curtis Weeks to life in prison because he spat at a prison guard.

_____ 15. Of thirty-two Liberals who sought re-election, thirty-one won.

Name _____ Date _____

EXERCISE 4-2

Weighing Evidence   *4a-2 (p. 124)*

Examine the following essay for the types of evidence supporting its assertions: facts, statistics, examples, expert opinions, and appeals to readers' beliefs or needs. Be prepared to point to at least one example of each and to evaluate it as accurate, relevant, representative, and adequate.

SORRY, SISTERS, THIS IS NOT THE REVOLUTION

Barbara Ehrenreich, *Time*

1   American feminism late 1980s style could be defined, cynically, as women's rush to do the same foolish and benighted things that have traditionally occupied men. And why not? The good and honest things that have traditionally occupied women—like rearing children and keeping husbands in clean shirts—are valued in the open market at somewhere near the minimum wage. And whatever one thinks of investment banking or corporate law, the perks and the pay are way ahead of those for waitressing and data entry. So, every time a woman breaks a new barrier the rest of us tend to cheer—even if she's running a pollution-producing company or toting a gun in some ill-considered war.

2   Two cheers, anyway. Because this is not the revolution that I, at least, signed on for. When the feminist movement burst forth a couple of decades ago, the goal was not just to join 'em—and certainly not just to beat 'em—but to improve an imperfect world. Gloria Steinem sketched out the vision in a 1970 TIME Essay titled "What It Would Be Like If Women Win." What it would be like was a whole lot better, for men as well as women, because, as she said right up front, "Women don't want to exchange places with men." We wanted *better* places, in a kinder, gentler, less rigidly gendered world.

3   We didn't claim that women were morally superior. But they had been at the receiving end of prejudice long enough, we

thought, to empathize with the underdog of either sex. Then too, the values implicit in motherhood were bound to clash with the "male values" of competitiveness and devil-may-care profiteering. We imagined women storming male strongholds and, once inside, becoming change agents, role models, whistle-blowers. The hand that rocks the cradle was sure to rock the boat.

4   To a certain extent, women have "won." In medicine, law and management, they have increased their participation by 300% to 400% since the early '70s, and no one can argue that they haven't made *some* difference. Women lawyers have spearheaded reforms in the treatment of female victims of rape and battering. Women executives have created supportive networks to help other women up the ladder and are striving to sensitize corporations to the need for flexible hours, child care and parental leave. Women journalists have fought to get women's concerns out of the "style section" and onto the front page. Women doctors, according to physician-writer Petri Klass, are less paternalistic than their male counterparts and "better at listening."

5   But, I'm sorry, sisters, this is not the revolution. What's striking, from an old-fashioned (ca. 1970) feminist perspective, is just how *little* has changed. The fact that law is no longer classified as a "nontraditional" occupation for women has not made our culture any less graspingly litigious or any more concerned with the rights of the underdog. Women doctors haven't made a dent in the high-tech, bottom-line fixation of the medical profession, and no one would claim that the influx of executive women has ushered in a new era of high-toned business ethics.

6   It's not that we were wrong back in the salad days of feminism about the existence of nurturant "feminine values." If anything, women have more distinctive views as a sex than they did 20 years ago. The gender gap first appeared in the presidential election of 1980, with women voting on the more liberal side. Recent polls show that women are more likely to favor social spending for the poor and to believe it's "very important" to work "for the betterment of American society."

7   So why haven't our women pioneers made more of a mark? Charitably speaking, it may be too soon to expect vast transformations. For one thing, women in élite, fast-track positions are still pathetically scarce. FORTUNE magazine found this past July that in the highest echelons of corporate managers, fewer than

one-half of 1% are female. Then there's the exhaustion factor. Women are far more likely to work a "double day" of career plus homemaking. The hand that rocks the cradle—and cradles the phone, and sweeps the floor, and writes the memo and meets the deadline—doesn't have time to reach out and save the world.

8   But I fear, too, that women may be losing the idealistic vision that helped inspire feminism in the first place. Granted, every Out group—whether defined by race, ethnicity or sexual preference— seeks assimilation as a first priority. But every Out group carries with it a critical perspective, forged in the painful experiences of rejection and marginalization. When that perspective is lost or forgotten, a movement stands in danger of degenerating into a scramble for personal advancement. We applaud the winners and pray that their numbers increase, but the majority will still be found far outside the gates of privilege, waiting for the movement to start up again.

9   And for all the pioneering that brave and ambitious women have done, the female majority remains outside, earning 70¢ to the man's $1 in stereotypically female jobs. That female majority must still find a way to survive the uncaring institutions, the exploitative employers and the deep social inequities the success-ful few have not yet got around to challenging.

10   Maybe, now that women have got a foot in the door, it's time to pause and figure out what we intend to do when we get inside. Equality with men is a fine ambition, and I'll fight for any woman's right to do any foolish or benighted thing that men are paid and honored for. But ultimately, assimilation is just not good enough. As one vintage feminist T shirt used to say, IF YOU THINK EQUALITY IS THE GOAL ... YOUR STANDARDS ARE TOO LOW.

EXERCISE 4-3

Discovering Assumptions   *4a-3 (p. 127)*

Analyse the following assertions to determine their underlying assumptions using the guidelines on page 128. Then decide whether those assumptions need the support of evidence. Your instructor may ask you to work with other classmates.

1. Murderers should pay for their crimes with their lives.

2. To vote for capital punishment is to vote for killing people.

3. Capital punishment is murder; it is the taking of human life.

4. Spanking is not an appropriate way for parents to discipline their children.

5. Spanking as a means of discipline gives children the message that hitting is okay.

6. There are better ways of disciplining children than spanking.

7. By donating to the Open Your Heart fund, you will ease the plight of hungry and homeless people in your locality.

8. Helping the hungry and homeless is a serious business.

9. We must act quickly to end the slaughter of dolphins.

10. No one knows how many dolphin kills have gone unreported.

EXERCISE 4-4

Identifying Logical Fallacies   *4b (p. 134)*

Identify the logical fallacies in the following sentences. Each sentence represents one or more of the evasion fallacies (begging the question, non sequitur, appealing to readers' fear or pity, bandwagon, flattery, argument ad populum, and argument ad hominem) or of the over-simplifications (hasty generalization, reductive fallacy, post hoc fallacy, either/or fallacy, and false analogy). Work with the "Checklist of fallacies" on page 135.

> *Example:* If El Salvador's government is overthrown, Costa Rica's will be next.
>
> *non sequitur*

1. Seat belts are unnecessary; I do not need the government's conscience in my car to make me a safe driver.

2. If young people just set their goals high and work hard, they'll have successful careers.

3. Bureaucrats are concerned only with putting in their time, not with serving the public.

4. How can anyone believe that a car made by dedicated Canadian workers in a Canadian factory is unsafe?

5. People who really know automobiles usually prefer British cars.

6. He must have been drinking, because he is always happy when he has been drinking, and he is happy now.

7. Jane is a lovely, gracious woman, but she has a very sharp business sense.

8. Cars wouldn't be so outrageously expensive if it weren't for all the unnecessary extras like pollution control devices, ignition locks, air bags, and padded dashboards.

9. If anything can go wrong, it will.

10. People's right to adequate medical care will be guaranteed only if the federal government reverses its decisions on health-care spending.

11. Be careful of your grammar when you talk to an English teacher, or you will be criticized.

12. If you want four more years of graft-free city government, re-elect Charles Brown as mayor.

13. How can I vote for Charles Brown for mayor when he just divorced his wife last year?

14. Most of the people I know in the fashionable areas of Toronto will be voting for him.

15. The game will be exciting because it is for the championship.

16. If scientists can send a spaceship to Mars, they should be able to cure the common cold.

17. Sky diving is just like roller skating—as long as you are careful, you will not get hurt.

18. So many workers belong to unions that high-quality work is rare.

19. If we don't build nuclear power plants, we will be forever dependent on imported oil.

20. Adults need discipline just as much as children do.

exer

4

49

Name _____ Date _____

EXERCISE 4-5

Analysing an Argument   *4g (p. 153)*

Analyse the following argument, answering these questions:

1. What is the thesis?
2. How is the argument organized?
3. What kinds of evidence does the writer use? As far as you can tell, is the evidence accurate, relevant, representative, and adequate?
4. In what ways does the writer accommodate reader needs?
5. What fallacies do you find?
6. What emotional appeals do you find?
7. How does the writer establish her ethical appeal?
8. How has the writer acknowledged the opposition?

After your initial analysis, your instructor may ask you to compare your findings with those of your classmates.

CAPITAL PUNISHMENT IS A CRIME

Natalie Crowns (student writer)

1   Capital punishment is a fancy phrase for legally killing people. It is a great evil—surely the greatest evil except for war.
Capital punishment is murder; it is the taking of human life, done
without any consideration for mothers, fathers, children, husbands, or wives. And the ones who make the decision to use the
death penalty are the very people we look to for protection. Of
course, there must be some measure of social revenge for a crime
that has been done. However, the killing of one human being as
punishment for the killing of another is every bit as violent and
immoral as the original act and does not serve as a deterrent to
future crimes.

2   A person's most profound emotional response to a murder is
to want the criminal to suffer as the victim did. Some argue that
retribution requires criminals to pay for their crimes with their

lives. An execution is positive proof that the bad guy is not getting away with the crime and that justice is served. A criminal who has violated the trust of a moral community has thereby injured it and must be punished for the sake of justice. However, taking of life because a wrongdoer deserves it is the total denial of the wrongdoer's dignity and worth.

3   What seems to be peculiarly cruel and horrible about capital punishment is that the condemned person has a period of waiting, knowing how and when she or he is to be killed, which itself is a source of moral suffering more terrible than death. Criminals usually do not warn their victims of the date when they will inflict a horrible death and from that moment onward confine these victims for months, even years. Such a monstrous act is not encountered in private life.

4   When a man is accused of throwing a child from a high rise terrace, society's emotional, hysterical response is that he should be given an opportunity to see how endless the seconds are from the thirty-first story to the ground. In a civilized society, however, that will never happen. And so people against capital punishment take the position that the death penalty is wrong not only because it consists of stooping to the level of the killers but because it is impossible for something as horrifying as what happened to the victims to happen to the killer; what people want in the death penalty, they will never get.

5   The death penalty is supposedly there to promote deterrence and bring retribution, but when the Supreme Court in the United States reviewed all the evidence for deterrence in 1976, it described that evidence as inconclusive. Studies in criminology have presented ample statistical and psychiatric evidence to show that most capital offences are not committed by the criminally minded, but as a result of a mental illness, an uncontrolled temper under some great provocation, and by sheer accident (Heline 37).

6   The only reason for a death penalty is to exact retribution. Is there anyone who really thinks that it is a deterrent, that there are considerable numbers of criminals who think twice about committing crimes because of the sentence involved? Most criminals believe that it is the other guy who will get caught or they'll bargain for a lesser sentence. In fact, the death penalty not only fails as a deterrent, but it actually increases the amount of violence in

society. Statistical evidence proves that widely publicized executions result in more murders rather than fewer (Heline 35).

7   And the death penalty has wider effects on society at large. When there is capital punishment, we are all involved in the horrible business of a long, premeditated killing, and most of us will to some degree share in the emotional response. The advocates of capital punishment do not take into consideration the effects of the execution on the family of the convicted person. They also forget about how the participants in an execution are turned into agents, not people. A priest stands by and certifies that it's a moral event. Witnesses make it a certified happening. A doctor swears death occurred humanely, on schedule, and completely. Yet the priest is dedicated to love, the warden is there to restrain people who have hurt other people, and the doctor is trained to save lives (Jackson and Christian 292).

8   Yet another problem with the death penalty is the possibility of mistakenly executing an innocent person, such as in the case of Timothy Evans. In 1950, Evans, who was of "limited intelligence and confessed to slaying his wife," later retracted his admission of guilt. He was executed anyway, and four years later another man confessed to the murder (Gettinger 184). The death penalty may also be used to discriminate against minorities and the mentally retarded.

9   The advocates of capital punishment can and do accentuate their arguments with descriptions of the awful physical details of such horrendous murders as those committed by Clifford Olson. All of us naturally respond to those atrocities with shock and horror, and rightly so. But executions are also too horrendous, and there are two important points to remember. First, the murders being described are not being done by us, or in our name, or with our approval; and our power to stop them is very limited. Every execution, on the other hand, is done by our paid servants, in our collective name, and we can stop them all. Secondly, the descriptions of murders are relevant to the subject of capital punishment only on the theory that two wrongs make a right, or that killing murderers can lessen their victims' sufferings or bring them back to life, or that capital punishment is the best deterrent to murder.

10   Is it morally legitimate for us to do in a state of calm reason what someone whose actions we have scorned and condemned did in a state of passion or in a condition of amorality or stupid-

ity? So far as moral reinforcement goes, the difference between life imprisonment and capital punishment is that imprisonment continues to respect the value of human life. The plain message of capital punishment, on the other hand, is that life ceases to be sacred whenever someone with the power to take it away decides to exercise that right.

11   For many people, capital punishment is a sanitized and symbolic issue: an eye for an eye, a tooth for a tooth. To vote for capital punishment is to vote to kill real, live people. "We have learned," said the Minister of Justice in Belgium, a country that abandoned capital punishment almost a century ago, "that the best means to teach respect for human life consists of refusing to take life in the name of the law" (Heline 37). The death penalty does no one in our society any good. It doesn't prevent death, and it does not make society better or nicer or satisfy any moral need. In fact, it perpetuates a faith in the effectiveness of violence as a solution to grim human problems.

Works Cited

Gettinger, Stephen H. *Sentenced to Die.* New York: Macmillan, 1979.

Heline, Theodore. *Capital Punishment: Historical Trends Toward Its Abolishment.* LaCanada, CA: New Age Press, 1965.

Jackson, Bruce, and Diane Christian. *Death Row.* Boston: Beacon, 1980.

Part II GRAMMATICAL SENTENCES

Chapter 5 *Understanding Sentence Grammar*

EXERCISE 5-1

Identifying Subjects and Predicates   *5a-1 (p. 159)*

Using vertical lines, divide each of the following sentences into subjects and predicates. All the words that help identify the subject are
part of the subject. Then on separate paper compose sentences that
follow the patterns of these sentences. Separate your subjects and
predicates with vertical lines.

> *Example:*   Dairy cows and beef cattle/graze along our highways.
>
> *White oaks and red oaks/grow side by side in our
> forests.*

1. The most common dairy cow in North America is the Holstein.

2. About 70 percent of the dairy cattle on this continent are
   Holsteins.

3. You have probably seen these large black-and-white cows grazing
   beside the highway.

4. The origin of this breed of cattle is Northern Europe, specifically
   Friesland, a province of the Netherlands.

5. They were later raised also in Holstein, an area of Germany.

6. Dutch settlers brought the first Holstein cattle to the United States in the early 1600s.

7. Somewhat smaller than Holsteins, Guernseys are a light brown, almost golden, with white markings.

8. These dairy cattle were developed on the Isle of Guernsey in the English Channel and did not arrive in North America until the early 1800s.

9. Jersey, another island in the English Channel, is the namesake of the Jersey cow.

10. The Jerseys migrated to that island across a land bridge from Europe.

11. Jersey cows are fawn-coloured and have an interesting muzzle: black encircled by a light ring.

12. These three breeds—Holsteins, Guernseys, and Jerseys—make up most of the milk-producing cattle in North America.

13. Their ability to produce large quantities of milk makes them popular with dairy producers.

EXERCISE 5-2

Identifying Nouns, Verbs, and Pronouns   *5a-2 (p. 159)*

In the following passages, identify all words functioning as nouns with **N**, all words functioning as verbs with **V**, and all pronouns with **P**. Sentences will often have more than one of each.

      N   V P V V   N

Example: Herb decided he had seen enough violence.

1   A cat makes a fine pet for a family. Two cats are even better because each entertains the other. But three or four cats are definitely too many cats. They are independent creatures and when you have more than two they think they own the house. They think they are kings and queens in a castle, lords and ladies with obedient servants who care for them. These obedient servants prepare meals at the appropriate times, groom them and clean the sanitary facilities. Meanwhile, the 'servants' who pay the taxes and buy the groceries wonder sometimes who is really in charge.

2 Another problem arises at the grocery store if you have four cats. Browsing the shelves for new delicacies to tempt the appetites of your finicky live-in guest, you begin to suspect everyone in the country must own a cat. On the other side of the aisle, where the dog food is kept, are bags upon bags and cans upon cans of food for "man's best friend." But here on the cat food side, the shelves are stripped nearly bare. So, you pick from the few items remaining on the shelves. For four cats, you need a cart full of cans and boxes of dry stuff; on the rack below, you stow the twenty-five pounds of litter. Proceeding to the checkout lane, you hope no one will notice the percentage of your entire grocery order devoted solely to cat supplies.

EXERCISE 5-3

Using Nouns and Verbs:
Writing Sentences   *5a (p. 158)*

The words shown below can be used as both nouns and verbs. For each word, first write a sentence using it as a noun and then write a sentence using it as a verb.

> *Example:* whistle   *Ruth carried a dog whistle on a chain around her neck.*
>
> *Ruth whistled for her dog.*

1. experiment

2. number

3. model

4. use

5. supply

6. form

7. surface

8. burn

9. note

10. count

exer
5

EXERCISE 5-4

Identifying Parts of the Sentence   *5a-3 (p. 163)*

The following sentences are grouped by pattern. Within each group, identify subjects, verbs, objects, and complements by writing the appropriate abbreviation above the word. Disregard modifiers.

Pattern 1: S, V

1. Bats live a long time.

2. Bamboo plants grow for many years without flowering.

3. Some fishes cluck, croak, or grunt.

4. Sound waves must travel through a medium.

5. Some unanswered questions about quark matter still remain.

Pattern 2: S, V, DO

6. Some foods may increase chances of getting cancer.

7. However, other foods may provide an effective means of preventing the disease.

8. Pandas eat almost nothing except bamboo.

9. Computer camps offer computer training in a camplike setting.

10. Scientists group butterflies into families according to their physical features.

Pattern 3: S, V, SC

11. Bats are intriguing creatures because of their unusual characteristics.

12. Freon is a common cooling agent.

13. The Doppler effect is an apparent change in pitch.

14. Infrasound means sound with frequencies below the range of human hearing.

15. The sun's rays are strongest between 10:00 A.M. and 2:00 P.M.

Pattern 4: S, V, IO, DO

16. A male frog sends a female frog a hoarse mating call.

17. Zoo officials sometimes must feed baby animals milk from a bottle.

18. Medical technologists very seldom give people high doses of ionizing radiation.

19. Trilobites have given paleontologists evidence of continent formation.

20. According to some botanists, trees sometimes send other trees chemical messages when under attack by insects.

Pattern 5: S, V, DO, OC

21. Scientists call butterflies and moths Lepidoptera.

22. They sometimes call computers "artificial intelligence."

23. Some botanists consider the Cretaceous period the time of the first flowers.

24. Environmentalists have declared the spread of airborne pollutants a major environmental concern.

25. Physicians have named some birth defects "fetal alcohol syndrome."

EXERCISE 5-5

Sentence Patterns: Combining Sentences   *5a-3 (p. 163)*

exer
5

Combine each group of sentences according to the designated sentence pattern. Omit all unnecessary repetitions, and do not alter meaning.

> *Example:* **subject   verb**
>
> El Salvador is in Central America.
>
> El Salvador is next to Guatemala.
>
> It is next to Honduras.
>
> *El Salvador is in Central America, next to Guatemala and Honduras.*

1. **subject   verb**

   Pyramids still stand today.

   The pyramids are Mayan.

   The pyramids are enormous.

2. **subject   verb   direct object**

   Mayan Indians settled El Salvador.

   Other Indian tribes settled El Salvador.

   They settled as early as 3000 B.C.

3. **subject**   **verb**   **subject complement**

El Salvador's climate is agreeable.

The average temperature ranges from 73 to 80 degrees Fahrenheit.

That is the year-round temperature.

4. **subject**   **verb**   **indirect object**   **direct object**

The climate gives El Salvadorans an opportunity.

They play soccer.

They play on soccer fields throughout the country.

5. **subject**   **verb**   **direct object**   **object complement**

Spain made the country a Spanish colony.

It happened in 1524.

EXERCISE 5-6

Adjectives and Adverbs:
Identifying Function   *5b-1 (p. 168)*

exer
5

In the following sentences, underline each word functioning as an adjective (modifying a noun) once and each word functioning as an adverb (modifying a verb, an adjective, or an adverb) twice. Then draw an arrow from the modifier to the word it modifies.

Example: Most people ordinarily assume that drinkable water will always be available to them.

1. Water conservation is becoming an urgent issue in North America.

2. Some areas of Canada have greater potential for water shortages, while others have abundant sources of drinkable water.

3. Alberta, Saskatchewan, and British Columbia are particularly vulnerable to relatively severe shortages.

4. As conflicts increase beween types of users, the situation becomes increasingly complex.

5. There are numerous reasons for these conflicts between withdrawal users and nonwithdrawal users.

6. People prefer to live and farm in the warmer, drier areas where they usually need to irrigate.

7. However, these irrigation needs conflict with plans for non-withdrawal uses, such as hydroelectric projects.

8. Sometimes the conflicts are between nonwithdrawal users, such as the hydroelectric projects, and water-dependent industries, such as salmon fisheries.

9. To make matters worse, various types of pollution are a growing problem.

10. The various pressures on the water supply are more serious in the United States.

11. Those serious pressures could affect Canada adversely in the future.

12. According to scientists, the average person uses approximately 140 gallons of water every day.

13. Furthermore, every day, each person in the United States contributes to 1400 more gallons used in agriculture and in industry.

14. One solution has been interbasin transfers from Canada to the United States, but these have been small-scale transfers so far.

15. Another solution scientists are investigating thoroughly is removal of salinity from ocean water.

16. Still another answer has been to dam rivers and divert the flow to needy areas.

17. Even aquifers, those underground rock formations that yield fresh, clean water to deep wells, are fast being depleted by overuse.

18. But getting potable water from places where it is plentiful to areas where it is scarce is a problem that has not been satisfactorily solved.

19. Neither have researchers discovered a practical and inexpensive way of desalinating seawater in amounts adequate to serve the need.

20. In the future, Canada's water supply may prove more attractive to the United States, and more agreements and protections will need to be put into place.

EXERCISE 5-7

Prepositional Phrases: Identifying Function *5c-1 (p. 170)*

In the following paragraph, enclose all the prepositional phrases in parentheses and draw an arrow from each preposition to the word the phrase modifies.

Example: The fence post was embedded (in a block) (of cement).

As you drive along the highway in the country, you often see beef cattle grazing in pastures. In contrast to dairy cows, which are raised for milk production, beef cattle are raised for their meat and are much larger. Three major breeds of beef cattle in Canada are the Shorthorn, the Black Angus, and the Hereford. The Shorthorn was the first to arrive in Canada in 1832, and is still popular because it can be used both for beef and milk. The Black Angus, or Aberdeen Angus, originated in eastern Scotland in the county of Angus. The Black Angus is readily identifiable by its smooth, black coat. It was first imported to North America in the late 1800s. Herefords were developed in Hertfordshire, England, and were also brought to North America in the 1800s. These beef cattle have white faces, reddish coats, and white markings. A very hardy breed, it quickly became Western Canada's main commercial breed. In addition to these major breeds of beef cat-

tle, two other types are Charolais and Redpoll. Charolais is a fairly

recent import, having come to this country in the latter part of this

century. The breed originated in France. Charolais cattle are white,

and they grow quite large, an adult bull being almost twice the size of

a Jersey milk cow, for example. The Redpoll, like the Shorthorn, is

used both for dairy and beef production. Continental breeds have

become quite popular in this century and are often used for cross-

breeding to strengthen herds.

EXERCISE 5-8

Using *-ing* and *-ed* Participles   *5c-2 (p. 173)*

Underline the appropriate participle in each sentence.

> *Example:*   Modern Canadian politics shows a (*surprised, surprising*) following for satirical political parties.

1. An (*interested, interesting*) political party from recent years is the Rhinoceros party.

2. (*Founded, founding*) in 1963, by Montreal doctor Jacques Ferron, the party has had no serious platform.

3. A (*surprised, surprising*) fact is that the Rhinoceros party fielded 89 candidates across Canada in 1984.

4. In fact, this largely (*unknown, unknowing*) party did receive 99 207 votes, or 0.79 percent of the total votes cast.

5. The (*guided, guiding*) principle of the party was to make fun of federal election campaigns.

6. Its goal was to combat (*interfered, interfering*) "serious" influences.

7. But members of the party could not agree on the (*burned, burning*) issue of what their platform was if they did get elected.

8. Many members of the Rhinoceros party saw their mandate as attempting to reconcile the (*separated, separating*) differences between political parties.

9. Although there were many (*committed, committing*) party members, the official party was dissolved after Ferron's death in May 1985.

10. However, others have recently revived the ideas behind the (*declined, declining*) party.

11. The power of this (*intrigued, intriguing*) kind of party has always been to put election excesses into perspective.

12. The most recent party, under an (*acquired, acquiring*) name of "The Natural Law Party," promotes Yogic 'flying' for political stability.

EXERCISE 5-9

Verbal Phrases: Identifying Function   *5c-2 (p. 173)*

Each of these sentences contains an italicized verbal phrase. On the line at the left, identify the type of phrase—participial (p), gerund (g), or infinitive (i). If the phrase functions as an adjective or an adverb, draw an arrow to the word it modifies. If it functions as a noun, indicate on the line whether it is subject (S), direct object (DO), subject complement (SC), or object of a preposition (OP).

> *Example:* ___*i DO*___ Reading before writing helps *me focus on an idea.*

_____ 1. Students asked *to write about how they write* say a variety of things.

_____ 2. Most agree that they must first have *something to write about.*

_____ 3. *Finding a subject of interest* is often the most difficult part.

_____ 4. Besides *being interested in the subject,* the writer must know something about it.

_____ 5. When *composing a personal experience essay,* writers often find that the words flow easily.

_____ 6. *Writing a research paper* is much more difficult.

_____ 7. Some students say that the hardest papers for *them to write* are reactions or responses to journal articles.

_____ 8. They are uncertain about the angle *to take in their response.*

_____ 9. When *writing research papers,* some students are more organized than others.

_____ 10. The organized students make note cards *to organize the information they have gathered* and use the cards as a guide for their writing.

_____ 11. Students differ on the usefulness of *writing an outline.*

_____ 12. Some students report that they make outlines *to organize their thoughts for any of their papers.*

_____ 13. They find it exciting *to write once without an outline.*

_____ 14. They begin by *putting down whatever they are thinking on the subject.*

_____ 15. Rereading what they've written lets *them see if the paper follows along logically.*

_____ 16. They make necessary changes, *adding needed details.*

_____ 17. Sometimes, *seeing irrelevancies,* they delete material.

_____ 18. Since errors are *to be expected when we write,* most writers make corrections at some point.

_____ 19. Some writers edit as they write, others *preferring to wait until they have stopped writing.*

_____ 20. The way students write is often determined by the subject and the amount of time they have for *writing the paper.*

EXERCISE 5-10

Using Verbal Phrases   *5c-2 (p. 173)*

Rewrite the following sentences by reducing the italicized words to verbal phrases as indicated. Be careful not to alter the meaning when you make your changes.

> *Example:* Thomas did a lot of extra reading *so that he would be prepared for the responsibility of his new puppy.* (infinitive)
>
> *Thomas did a lot of extra reading to be prepared for the responsibility of his new puppy.*

1. Ever since *he played with his friend's dog, Blue,* he wanted a dog of his own. (gerund)

2. He didn't realize at first *the preparation* would be so time consuming. (gerund)

3. In his reading he learned that puppies *that are trained early* make better pets. (participle)

4. The puppy obedience classes *that are offered by various pet supply stores* seemed a logical choice. (participle)

5. He registered his new puppy in a six-week course *so that he could make the training easy and fun.* (infinitive)

6. *Because he interacted with many other puppies and their owners in the class,* he was sure his dog would also be well socialized. (participle)

7. After the formal part of the class, Thomas could also talk to the instructor *so that he could get more individual help.* (infinitive)

8. *Before he tried any of the techniques at home,* he made sure he had a variety of treats to reward the dog. (gerund)

9. He taught the dog *that it should sit, stay or lie down if he used certain hand signals.* (infinitive and participle)

10. The instructor *who was teaching the class* emphasized firmness and consistency. (participle)

EXERCISE 5-11

Subordinate Clauses: Identifying Function   *5c-4 (p. 179)*

exer
5

Each of these sentences has one subordinate clause, italicized. On the line at the left, tell the function of the clause—adjective (adj), adverb (adv), or noun (n). If the clause functions as an adjective or an adverb, draw an arrow to the word it modifies. If it functions as a noun, indicate on the line whether it is subject (S), direct object (DO), subject complement (SC), or object of a preposition (OP).

> *Example:* __*adv*__ Acquaintance rapes will not end *unless "no" really*
>
> *comes to mean "no."*

_____ 1. Colleges and universities have become concerned about *how to prevent date and gang rapes.*

_____ 2. Rape occurs *whenever a person is intimidated into submitting to sexual intercourse.*

_____ 3. Some surveys show *that 25 percent of women on campuses report having had sex against their wills.*

_____ 4. Other surveys show rates *that are much higher.*

_____ 5. Perhaps women *who are attending college and university today* are more willing to report such abuse than in the past, or the incidence may actually be increasing.

_____ 6. The attitude of some males is *that a date "owes" them a sexual encounter.*

_____ 7. Universities have begun campaigns *that combat such an attitude.*

_____ 8. Some of these moves come from campus administrators *who institute educational programs.*

_____ 9. Sometimes fraternities are the ones *who make the first move.*

_____ 10. Rape prevention workshops are one means *that has been adopted.*

_____ 11. Another is educational brochures *which have been pre-pared and circulated by fraternities, sororities, on-campus groups, and university administrators.*

_____ 12. These methods are aimed at changing attitudes, but, *even though these efforts may make some difference,* attitudes change slowly.

_____ 13. In the United States, California made an attempt to has-ten change *when the legislature adopted a resolution sug-gesting college suspension or expulsion of perpetrators.*

_____ 14. New York also has taken a stand against campus rape by appointing a governor's task force on rape and sexual assault, *which recommended adoption of prevention pro-grams at the state and city of New York universities.*

_____ 15. The real test of these measures is *whether they are effective in deterring campus rapes.*

77

EXERCISE 5-12

Sentence Combining: Subordinate Clauses   *5c-4 (p. 179)*

Combine each of the following pairs of sentences by making one of the sentences in each pair into a subordinate clause. Use the connector shown in parentheses and omit any words that are unnecessary in the combined sentence. Use correct punctuation as described in 5c-4.

> *Example:*   One Canadian newspaper is the *Globe and Mail.*
> Its daily publication and magazines are found in homes around the world. *(whose)*
>
> *One Canadian newspaper whose daily publication and magazines are found in homes around the world is the Globe and Mail.*

1. It first came out in 1844. *(when)*
   The *Globe* was initially a party journal.

2. It was rather modest in its beginnings. *(though)*
   It quickly became required reading for the business and cultural community.

3. George Brown began the paper with the support of a group of Reformers.
   He was its first editor. *(who)*

4. By 1876, Brown was sending the paper on early morning trains to Hamilton and London.
   He absorbed the mailing costs. *(who)*

5. Just after the beginning of this century, the *Globe* editors attempted to get national readership.
   They added "Canada's National Newspaper" to its masthead. *(who)*

6. By the late 1900s, the *Globe* had added drawings and photoengravings. *(although)*
   The quality of the reporting and editorials were the real reasons the newspaper succeeded.

7. The *Globe* wanted to expand into all parts of the country. *(because)*
   It merged with the *Mail and Empire* in 1936.

8. The *Mail and Empire* was also formed by the union of two papers.
   They were both Conservative. *(which)*

9. The *Mail* began as an independent Conservative party paper in 1872. *(although)*
It absorbed the *Empire*, another Conservative newspaper in 1895.

exer
5

10. The *Globe and Mail* has become Canada's only national daily paper.
It became the flagship of FP Publications' chain of newspapers in the 1960s. *(since)*

11. Many skilled journalists have worked on the *Globe and Mail*.
It had a circulation of more than 320 000 in the late 80s. *(which)*

12. It appears early in the morning. *(since)*
It is beamed by satellite to printing facilities across the country.

13. The newspaper boasts staff reporters based in locations around the world.
Many of them began their careers in Canadian cities. *(whom)*

14. Did you know?

    Two of the most famous *Globe and Mail* journalists are Jeffrey Simpson and John Fraser. *(that)*

exer

5

15. We might wonder about this.

    It is useful to know the origin of newspapers when we don't have any idea where their political ideology comes from. *(whether)* (the meaning changes)

EXERCISE 5-13

Using Subordinate Clauses   *5c-4 (p. 179)*

In the following sentences, underline each subordinate clause and circle each subordinating word (subordinating conjunction or relative pronoun). Then compose a complete sentence of your own that uses the same subordinating word. Underline the subordinate clauses and circle the subordinating words in your sentences.

> *Example:*   Elephants never forget (how) a trainer treats them.
>
>   *Charlene doesn't remember (how) she made the cookies.*

1. Renee did not stop crying until the ceremony ended.

2. Adam jogged through the park while his cat loped behind.

3. Pedestrians are increasingly menaced by bicyclists who ride on sidewalks.

4. If the dog is not confined, it will chew on the saplings.

5. I would have passed the test if I had understood the question.

6. Whatever money remains goes to the children's home.

7. We will put off our trip to Ottawa until the tulips are in bloom.

8. I knew that I should not have eaten so much.

9. The tenants, who complained regularly, found no remedy.

10. The council decided against establishing a dress code because so many students protested.

11. People who complain all the time never have time to smile.

12. The surprise is that the mayor was not convicted sooner.

EXERCISE 5-14

Compound Constructions:
Combining Words and Phrases   *5d-1 (p. 186)*

The following pairs of sentences are wordy and repetitious. Rewrite each of them into a single main clause by compounding words and phrases. Since the coordinating conjunction will not be joining main clauses, it should *not* be preceded by a comma.

> *Example:*   Weather forecasters rely on observation. They rely on an understanding of climatic behaviour.
>
> *Weather forecasters rely on observation and an understanding of climatic behaviour.*

1. To forecast weather, meteorologists must know present conditions. They must know past conditions.

2. Weather forecasting requires basic knowledge of how the atmosphere works. It requires knowledge of how weather systems are formed.

3. The sun's rays strike the earth at a 90-degree angle at the equator. They strike the earth at acute angles at the poles.

4. Much of the sun's energy is absorbed by the earth. This energy is changed into heat.

5. The amount of heat determines whether a 'front' is warm or cold. It determines the kind of precipitation.

6. Precipitation is water droplets that fall to earth. Precipitation is ice crystals that fall to earth.

7. Clouds precede the arrival of a warm front. Steady rain or snow precedes the arrival of a warm front.

8. Upcoming weather is dependent on the temperature of a front. It is dependent on the air pressure and relative humidity.

9. High-pressure winds blow clockwise in the Northern Hemisphere. They blow counterclockwise in the Southern Hemisphere.

10. Meteorologists use barometers for measuring air pressure. They use hygrometers for measuring relative humidity.

EXERCISE 5-15

Compound Constructions:
Using Clauses   *5d-1, 2 (pp. 186-190)*

Make two kinds of compound sentences by joining the following pairs of sentences *twice*, first with coordinating conjunctions and then with conjunctive adverbs. Try to use the most appropriate connectors. Remember that coordinating conjunctions should be preceded by commas; conjunctive adverbs that begin their clauses should be preceded by semicolons.

> *Example:* People experiencing the heat of summer often yearn for relaxation in the cool north woods. They begin packing their bags for the Muskoka lakes area.
>
> *People experiencing the heat of summer often yearn for relaxation in the cool north woods, so they begin packing their bags for the Muskoka lakes area.*
>
> *People experiencing the heat of summer often yearn for relaxation in the cool north woods; then they begin packing their bags for the Muskoka lakes area.*

1. The permanent population of the Muskoka lakes area is concentrated in Huntsville. Gravenhurst and Bracebridge are also centres for the permanent population.

2. In summer the Muskoka lakes attract swimmers and boaters. In winter they attract iceboaters and snowmobilers.

3. The Muskoka area has attracted visitors with its scenic splendour since Victorian times. The beauty of the rock and pine landscape and the clear lakes attracts many visitors still today.

4. The earliest vacation accommodations were luxury resort hotels. The hotels offered dance halls, croquet lawns, tennis courts, and tea rooms.

5. The first private cottages appeared in the late 19th century. They were built as summer homes on Lake Joseph.

6. At first Muskoka holidays were only available to the wealthy. The summer homes were owned mostly by wealthy Torontonians.

7. The Muskoka vacation is now available to all income brackets. There are facilities ranging from camping grounds to luxury hotels.

8. The area has roughly 20 000 vacation homes now. Over half of these homes still belong to Torontonians.

9. Many tourists from all over North America come to the Muskoka lakes area in the summer. Even more popular than the summer cottage, for the foreign visitor, are the campsites and the resorts.

10. Tourism is the biggest growth industry in the area. Most of the land is not suitable for agriculture and the lumber industry is only of local importance today.

EXERCISE 5-16

Order of Sentences:
Rewriting Sentences

5e (p. 190)

Rewrite the passive sentences to active voice and the inverted sentences to normal order. Be careful to keep meaning and verb time the same.

Examples: Some people are intimidated by computer technology.

Computer technology intimidates some people.

There are some people who are afraid to use computers.

Some people are afraid to use computers.

Change from passive to active.

1. Computers have been accepted as a part of everyday life.

2. Computer specialists are called on to assist decision makers.

3. The speed of computer transactions has come to be expected by almost everyone.

4. Long-distance telephone calls are completed by computers in a matter of seconds.

5. Airline and other reservations are made almost immediately by computers.

Change from inverted to normal order.

6. It is easy to forget what life was like before computers.

7. There are inexpensive computer programs being marketed.

8. There are some programs that are still costly.

9. It is programs like these that are newer and more specialized.

10. There are many people who depend on computers for survival on the job.

EXERCISE 5-17

Writing Compound, Complex,
and Compound-Complex Sentences   *5f (p. 194)*

The sentences below have structures that are compound, complex, or compound-complex. Observe the structure of each one; then write a sentence of your own that uses the same clause pattern. Use the same conjunctions or different ones.

> *Example:*   *(complex)* Some of the most familiar stories are fables that originated many centuries ago.
>
> *The limerick is a humorous verse that is often rib-ald and erotic.*

1. *(complex)* The fable is an ancient mode of instruction that takes the form of a story narrative.

2. *(complex)* It is somewhat like a tale because it tells a story and somewhat like a parable because it conveys a hidden meaning.

3. *(complex)* But the fable is unlike both tale and parable in that its primary purpose is moral instruction.

4. *(compound)* The fable seeks improvement in human conduct, but it conceals this purpose within the tale.

5. *(compound-complex)* A fable anthropomorphizes animals and plants when it endows them with personalities and motivations, and in so doing it indirectly instructs the audience about its morality.

6. *(compound-complex)* A fabulist, or a person who writes fables, advises audiences about their behaviour; at the same time, the fabulist avoids directly telling audiences that their behaviour needs improving.

7. *(complex)* Besides instructing an audience on moral improvement, the fabulist sometimes draws attention to praiseworthy behaviour that others might seek to emulate.

8. *(compound)* The fabulist uses anthropomorphism effectively; another tool for creating a fable is humour.

9. *(complex)* One of the most famous fabulists was Aesop, an ancient Greek who wrote his fables in the sixth century B.C.

10. *(compound)* One of Aesop's most famous fables is "The Fox and the Grapes"; another is "The Tortoise and the Hare."

Chapter 6   Case of Nouns and Pronouns

EXERCISE 6-1

Using Pronoun Case   *6a-h (pp. 196-205)*

A. Change the following statements to questions that begin with *who* or *whom* as replacements for the underlined words.

Example: <u>Professor Rogers</u> will be teaching this class.

Who will be teaching this class?

1. The new dean will be <u>Dr. Brown.</u>

2. This car belongs to <u>Mr. Jackson.</u>

3. <u>Kathryn</u> plans to drive to Winnipeg.

4. We can count on <u>Jacob and Sarah</u> to work at the hospital.

5. I can ask <u>Mr. Schwartz</u> about organic gardening.

6. <u>Brad</u> was the last person to leave the room.

7. I should call <u>Mrs. Shipman</u> if I'm delayed.

8. Applicants should send their cheques to <u>John Iverson.</u>

9. We can ask <u>George</u> to make the sign.

10. <u>Everyone</u> has read the assigned chapter.

B. In the sentences below, cross out each underlined noun (or phrase) and substitute an appropriate pronoun.

Example: The committee should have appointed ~~Kevin~~ *him* and me.

1. The handmade ornament is one donated by <u>Diane</u> and me.

2. I am not as smart as <u>Peter,</u> but my grades are just as good.

3. <u>Elizabeth</u> and Karen were born on the same day.

4. It must have been <u>the students in Mrs. Linden's class</u> who left the books.

5. The dispute was between <u>Jim</u> and the clerk.

6. <u>My sister and my brother</u> bought a tape deck.

7. Hardly any love remains between <u>Beth</u> and me.

exer
6

8. After practice, the batboy brought <u>Janet</u> and me cold drinks.

9. <u>Julie</u> and the teacher disagreed over the grade.

10. We expected <u>Michael</u> to win, not Delgado.

11. The winning chess players—<u>Andrew</u> and you—will get free tickets to the concert.

12. No one is more deserving than you and <u>Andrew</u>.

13. I've selected the other members of the group—you and <u>Pablo.</u>

14. Ingrid cannot play chess as well as <u>Andrew</u> and you.

15. The game was well played by <u>Luis</u> as well as by Ines.

C. Circle the correct pronoun in each pair below.

Example: ((We,) Us) math majors are required to take the class.

1. I explained to the policeman, "I'd appreciate *(you, your)* giving me just a warning."

2. The bank would not grant *(we, us)* fraternity members a loan.

3. Show the map to *(whoever, whomever)* plans to drive.

4. *(We, Us)* students all get discounts.

5. John is stronger than either Larry or *(I, me)*.

6. Chris tells old jokes to *(whoever, whomever)* will listen.

7. The two latecomers, Judith and *(I, me)*, agreed on who would do the work.

8. *(We, Us)* freshmen no longer are subject to hazing from sopho-mores.

9. Between you and *(I, me)*, I think the play was a flop.

10. *(Who, Whom)* did you meet in the library?

EXERCISE 6-2

Pronoun Case: Review   *6a-h (pp. 196-205)*

Rewrite this short narrative, changing the beginning sentence to read as follows:

That morning Colleen decided that her rabbit needed some attention.

Then, as you rewrite, change all first-person *I* references to third-person pronouns referring to Colleen: *she* and *her*. Where necessary, repeat *Colleen*. When you finish, the narrative will describe something Colleen did rather than something the writer did.

That morning I decided that my rabbit needed some attention. So far that winter, Edmonton had accumulated nineteen inches of snow on the ground, with drifts and piles of shovelled snow much higher. Because of the high winds overnight, all my previous tracks through the yard were filled in. But the bunny, for whom I was feeling particularly sorry that day, had no food, no hay, and only ice in place of water. So I plunged out into the drifts, plodding through snow several inches above my knees.

First I had to get some hay from under the porch. My pulling and tearing at the hay from the bale might have sent me flat into the snow if the drifts hadn't been packed around my legs so tightly that they held me up. Next was the matter of getting myself and the hay across the yard to the rabbit hutch. The hay survived better than I. Except for a few bits trailing across the yard, it arrived intact. I, however, had snow packed on my jeans and into my boots.

The next task was for me to lift the cover of the rabbit hutch, snow and all. As I struggled, I was thinking about the eight-year-old bunny, and I half expected to find him in a corner, stiff and feet up. But as I raised the lid, sliding the snow off onto the ground and tossing the hay inside, out from his enclosed, insulated house hopped old Checker, ready to begin another day. I removed the icy food and water dishes and trekked back over the yard and into the basement to fill them. My trip back to the hutch wasn't any easier than the first one, for this time I was carrying a sloshing water dish in one snow-encrusted glove and the pellet-filled food dish in the other. But Checker and I were both glad when I managed to get most of the water and food out there— he definitely more than I. I myself was a lot gladder when I had my cold, wet jeans off and had put something warm and dry on my legs and feet. For Checker and me, that was enough snow adventuring for one day.

Chapter 7 Verb Forms, Tense, Mood, and Voice

EXERCISE 7-1

Identifying the Principal Parts
of Irregular Verbs   *7a (p. 208)*

Circle the correct form of the verb from each pair in parentheses. On the lines following, fill in the principal parts (infinitive, past tense, and past participle) of the correct verb. If necessary, consult a dictionary or the list of irregular verbs on pages 200-202.

Example: I had to *(lie, lay)* down. ___*lie*___ ___*lay*___ ___*lain*___

1. The cold wind *(blowed, blew)* up   _____ _____ _____
   the alley.

2. Jerry had *(wrote, written)* down   _____ _____ _____
   the directions.

3. The professor *(began, begun)* the   _____ _____ _____
   class with a joke.

4. He had *(ran, run)* the mile in   _____ _____ _____
   record time.

5. Interest rates on student loans   _____ _____ _____
   have *(raised, risen)*.

6. She *(drunk, drank)* Gatorade   _____ _____ _____
   during the game.

7. He *(drove, drived)* the golf ball   _____ _____ _____
   250 yards.

8. She had not *(given, gave)* a minute   _____ _____ _____
   of her time.

9. The problem of boarding the dog had not *(come, came)* up before.   _____ _____ _____

10. The book had *(laid, lain)* on the shelf for many years.   _____ _____ _____

11. She *(finded, found)* the gift on her pillow.   _____ _____ _____

12. The team had *(swum, swam)* an hour that morning.   _____ _____ _____

13. They *(knew, knowed)* that the class was easy.   _____ _____ _____

14. The cat *(bitten, bit)* him on the wrist.   _____ _____ _____

15. They had *(ate, eaten)* before going out.   _____ _____ _____

16. He is *(suppose, supposed)* to arrive Monday.   _____ _____ _____

17. Wilson *(brung, brought)* a guest along.   _____ _____ _____

18. The platter *(broke, breaked)* when it hit the floor.   _____ _____ _____

19. They *(flew, flied)* in from Ottawa.   _____ _____ _____

20. The patient had *(went, gone)* to the examination room.   _____ _____ _____

21. The balloon had *(burst, bursted)* against the power lines.   _____ _____ _____

22. The skunk has *(become, became)* Denny's favourite pets.   _____ _____ _____

23. The attorney *(proved, proven)* his case.   _____ _____ _____

24. No problem with cheating has *(arose, arisen)*.   _____ _____ _____

25. Someone has *(sat, set)* on Martha's broken chair. _____ _____ _____

26. May and Raymond have *(took, taken)* the train. _____ _____ _____

27. The driver *(swore, sweared)* at the pedestrian. _____ _____ _____

28. I *(use, used)* to know someone named John Smith. _____ _____ _____

29. We *(seen, saw)* the accident on our way home. _____ _____ _____

30. The shortstop *(throwed, threw)* him out. _____ _____ _____

EXERCISE 7-2

Using the -s Forms of Verbs   *7c (p. 212)*

Rewrite the following paragraphs, placing the action in the present. Begin by changing the first sentence to read:

Today Beverly learns something about writing.

Then, as you rewrite, change verbs as necessary to describe the action as if it were happening right now. Use the *-s* forms, not the *-ing* forms.

Last week Beverly learned something about writing. She learned that writing is a way of thinking, a way of learning. Her teacher quoted somebody: "How can I know what I think until I see what I say?" Beverly discovered that she learned when she wrote.

Her teacher asked the class to write about whether the government should pay for all education, including university. Beverly had never thought about that subject before, and she wondered what to say about it. But she started writing, and soon she had written several paragraphs in which she stated that students should take the responsibility for their own education and that this responsibility did not happen if somebody else paid for that education.

Suddenly Beverly understood how people could learn through writing. When she was required to put some thoughts down on paper, she began thinking about things she had never thought about before. And by writing down those thoughts, she remembered them longer.

EXERCISE 7-3

Using the -*ed* Forms of Verbs   *7c (p. 212)*

Rewrite the following short essay to read as if the writer were recount-ing experiences in the past. Your first sentence will read:

When I learned to write, my dictionary was a close companion.

As you rewrite the essay, you will need to change all verbs to the past tense, in many cases using -*ed* forms. Avoid using *would* or *used to* with the verbs.

When I write, my dictionary is a close companion. I refer to it throughout the writing process for several purposes. Before I start writing, I often look up the meaning of a key word so that I clearly understand my subject. At that time I also locate related words and check their meanings.

I probably refer to the dictionary least while I carry out the actual writing. At that time my writing so absorbs my thoughts that I over-look spelling and, when I can't think of the right word, I use any word that comes close in meaning. I place a mark in the margin as a reminder to myself that I need to find a different word later.

After I affix my last period, I prepare to dig into my dictionary. Then I ask myself if each word I use is appropriate for my meaning. If I have any doubt, I look up the word and check its meaning. At that point, I also investigate other words given as synonyms; if they seem better than the ones I have, I use them instead. As I revise, I also check the spellings of words I'm not sure about.

My final use for the dictionary occurs when I am writing the final draft. I need to know how to divide words at the ends of lines. My dictionary has little dots between syllables to tell me where the syllables divide. Because my dictionary is so useful to me while I write, I keep it handy all the time.

exer

7

EXERCISE 7-4

Using Helping Verbs and Main Verbs   7d (p. 213)

Underline the correct words in parentheses.

Example: A clown might *(making, make)* people laugh.

1. Have you ever *(considering, considered)* being a clown?

2. I mean a clown whose face has been *(paint, painted)* all funny.

3. Clowns can *(entertained, entertain)* children in schools and hospitals.

4. They might also *(work, working)* in circuses.

5. To have a clown face, you must *(start, started)* with white makeup.

6. After you *(had covered, have covered)* your face with white makeup, you go to the next step.

7. You should *(applied, apply)* white talcum powder over the white makeup.

8. To finish your face, you should *(use, used)* red and black makeup.

9. A good professional clown will *(colour, colours)* only the mouth and nose and will *(make, makes)* only one or two other marks.

10. Children are sometimes *(scare, scared)* when clowns make up their faces too much.

11. Clowns who *(been, have been)* working as clowns for years have other advice too.

12. They *(be recommending, recommend)* that you not make up your upper lip.

13. Mouth expressions *(made, are made)* by the lower lip.

14. Making up the lower lip *(exaggerates, has exaggerating)* the expressions.

15. After you have *(painting, painted)* your face, you are ready to be a clown.

EXERCISE 7-5

Using Sequence of Tenses   *7f (p. 221)*

Rewrite the following paragraphs to read as if Suki lived in the past. Your first sentence should read:

Suki always knew precisely how to annoy someone.

As you rewrite, change the verbs so that they are in the appropriate sequence.

    Suki always knows precisely how to annoy someone. Suki is a cat, a regal blend of Siamese and Persian, two breeds that guarantee snobbery. This particular cat knows exactly when to come asking for food—just when the other cats have already been fed and the food has been put away. She understands precisely when to want to go into a room—just when the door has been closed. She is uncanny at knowing exactly where to sit—right in front of the dust mop or, more unerringly annoying, right on the dirt already swept together.

    Suki has a way of meowing that is meant to be especially irritating. The sound she makes is not a sweet little "mew" or a lusty "meow" or a pitiful "oh-h-h." Her utterance is more of a noisy complaint, a loud "ow-ow-ow!!" She makes this sound only when she thinks there's no one in sight but is still within hearing distance. Her other complaint, which comes when someone bumps her off the pile of dirt she's sitting on or won't open a door for her, is a cat sound that in human terms comes out something like "I can do whatever I want."

Suki obviously thinks she is queen of the house and whatever she does is her right and privilege.

EXERCISE 7-6

Writing Verb Tenses   *7f (p. 221)*

Underline the verbs in the following sentences. Then rewrite each sentence twice, changing the verb to the tenses indicated in parentheses.

> *Example:* Sometimes an element of truth <u>evolves</u> into a gross untruth.
>
> *(past)* *Sometimes an element of truth evolved into a gross untruth.*
>
> *(future)* *Sometimes an element of truth will evolve into a gross untruth.*

1. Scientific truth about the human brain has led to untrue assumptions.

   (past)

   (present)

2. One misinterpretation is that artistic, or visual, ability exists only in the right half of the brain.

   (past, past)

   (present perfect, present)

3. People assumed, falsely, that only the left half of the brain took on analytical, logical tasks and only the right half creative and visual work.

(present, present)

(past perfect, past)

4. But further research has shown the left brain to be just as perceptive visually as the right brain.

(present)

(past)

5. The primary distinction between the two halves of the brain is that the left brain controls language.

(present perfect, present)

(past, past)

6. In most people, only the left brain has the ability to name objects.

(past)

(past perfect)

7. The right brain recognizes those objects but doesn't have a name for them.

(present perfect, present)

(past perfect, past)

8. The left brain and right brain are connected to one another by the corpus callosum, a thick band of nerve fibres.

(future)

(future perfect)

9. Through this bundle of nerves, the two halves of the brain send information to one another.

(future)

(present perfect)

10. Because of this connection, it is a misinterpretation of scientific evidence to call a person "left-brained" or "right-brained."

(present perfect)

(future)

EXERCISE 7-7

Using Subjunctive Verb Forms   7g (p. 227)

Rewrite the following sentences, changing each italicized verb to a subjunctive form.

   Example: If that *was* the case, he would have protested.

   If that were the case, he would have protested.

1. The assignment sheet requires that each student *writes* a research paper.

2. If she *was* wise, she would take a mathematics course this term.

3. If the storm *was* to cause a blackout, we would be in trouble.

4. The requirement is that he *pays* before entering.

5. If the tax *was* repealed, the city would go bankrupt.

6. His mouth moved as if he *was* speaking.

7. If I *was* certain I could get a job in the space industry, I would major in engineering.

8. If the class president *was* elected by popular vote instead of selected by the teacher, the outcome would be more democratic.

EXERCISE 7-8

Verb Forms, Tense, and Mood   *7e-g (pp. 218-228)*

In the following paragraph, cross out any errors in verb forms, tense, or mood. Then write the correct verb above the error.

Nothing went right in my attempt to have a job interview last week. The interviewer had wrote me a letter requesting that I am on time; he also give me directions on how to get to his company. But I lost the directions, so when I was near the city, I begun looking for a service station where I could ask the way. Suddenly I hear a grinding noise coming from the right wheel. Since I knew something was broke or was about to break, I pull off the road. I knew I should of had the car inspected before the trip, but I had chose to put off the inspection so I will have money for the trip to the city. A police officer called a tow truck for me. Fortunately, I had brung along a credit card, so I could pay for the repair. When I be ready to leave, I ask the mechanic for directions. I found the company easily, but I was three hours late. The interviewer had went home, so I had drove all that way for nothing.

EXERCISE 7-9

Using the Active and Passive Voices 7h (p. 229)

Some of the sentences in the following passage are ineffective because of their passive constructions. Draw a line through those sentences and rewrite them in the active voice. The sentences with active verbs can remain as they are.

> *Example:* ~~Eating disorders are experienced by many people, especially young women.~~
>
> *Many people, especially young women, experience eating disorders.*

1   Bulimia is an eating disorder common to an estimated 18 percent of females in high school and college. People with this binge-and-purge disorder consume large amounts of junk food and then force themselves to vomit it up. Sometimes laxatives or diuretics are taken as a means of purging the body. Usually the bingeing is done in secret because the bulimics are ashamed of their habit. Yet the bingeing and purging are usually repeated as a result of the young woman's conviction that she is fat.

2   Only in recent years has bulimia been described in medical journals separately from another eating disorder, anorexia nervosa. Since 1980, bulimia has been considered a psychiatric illness. However, even though the causes of the bingeing and then

purging are psychiatric, the effects of the purging are largely physical.

3   The amount of an essential chemical in the body, potassium, is reduced by frequent purging of the body with vomiting, laxatives, or diuretics. Muscle weakness, even paralysis and kidney disease, may be caused by insufficient potassium. Other possible effects are damage to the esophagus and stomach, resulting in ulcers, stomach and throat pain, and difficulty in breathing. Even the teeth may be affected because of the acidity of the stomach fluids.

4   Treatment of bulimia usually involves both medical doctors and psychiatrists. Hospitalization is sometimes recommended, and treatment may last for months and years. The disorder can often be prevented with early medical consultation.

EXERCISE 7-10

Using Gerunds and Infinitives as Appropriate *7i (p. 232)*

Fill each blank with an infinitive or a gerund as appropriate.

   Example: Thomas promised *to return (return)* the book.

1. Miguel enjoyed _____ *(attend)* the art show.

2. He liked it so much he wanted _____ *(go)* back again.

3. But Anna persuaded him _____ *(wait)* a few days.

4. She reminded him that he risked _____ *(fail)* his history exam.

5. Miguel reluctantly agreed _____ *(wait)* until after the exam.

6. Mrs. Wang instructed five-year-old Angela _____ *(leave)* the table.

7. Angela had not yet finished _____ *(eat)*.

8. But she was having a temper tantrum and refused _____ *(eat)* her vegetables.

9. Her father ordered her _____ *(go)* to her room until she was ready to eat.

10. He hoped she would appreciate _____ *(have)* good food to eat.

11. Patrick decided _____ *(buy)* a computer.

12. He wanted _____ (use) it mainly for word processing.

13. But he also planned _____ (practise) his statistics on it.

14. He hoped _____ (get) his equipment for under $2000.

15. He invited his friend Charlie _____ (help) him shop for it.

16. They discussed _____ (go) to a computer store or a discount electronics store.

17. They both admitted not _____ (know) much about computers.

18. In the end, they delayed _____ (make) a decision until they got more information.

EXERCISE 7-11

Understanding Two-Word Verbs   *7j (p. 234)*

In the blank spaces at the left, substitute synonyms for the italicized two-word verbs. Use your dictionary as necessary.

Example: *Completing* Filling out forms is a necessary part of
          school registration.

_____ 1. Yung Lam *ran across* something interesting yesterday.

_____ 2. It happened when he was *looking over* his English assignment.

_____ 3. He was checking his spelling before *handing* the paper *in*.

_____ 4. He wanted to *clean up* all his errors.

_____ 5. But he also *found out* something new.

_____ 6. His rereading *brought up* a new idea.

_____ 7. He was surprised when the reading *brought* it *up*.

_____ 8. He decided that he would have to *think* it *over*.

_____ 9. He wondered if he should *write* the paper *over*.

_____ 10. The problem was that he had *left out* an important point.

_____ 11. He finally decided that he would not need to *throw* the paper *away*.

_____ 12. He could *fill in* a new paragraph to cover the omitted point.

_____ 13. Then he could *hand* the paper *in* knowing it was the best he could do.

_____ 14. He *called up* the paper on his word processor and made the changes.

Chapter 8   Agreement

EXERCISE 8-1

Subjects and Verbs   *8a (p. 237)*

In these sentences, the subjects are underlined once and the verbs twice. If a verb agrees with its subject, mark the sentence *C* on the line to the left. If a verb does not agree with its subject, cross out the verb and write the correct form on the line.

> *Example:*   _are_   There ~~is~~ three <u>problems</u> to work out before we can proceed.

_____ 1. The <u>difference</u> between twins <u>are</u> often surprising.

_____ 2. Both the <u>drinks</u> and the <u>dessert</u> <u>was</u> left off the bill.

_____ 3. <u>Each</u> of the puzzles <u>require</u> thirty minutes to solve.

_____ 4. <u>Neither</u> of us <u>enjoy</u> the outdoors.

_____ 5. There <u>is</u> only three original <u>songs</u> in the band's repertoire.

_____ 6. The <u>price</u> of every one of the houses in our neighbourhood <u>is</u> beyond our reach.

_____ 7. The <u>cabinet</u> for the stereo components <u>are</u> made of oiled oak.

_____ 8. The <u>subject</u> I want to write about <u>are</u> the effects of acid rain on the environment.

_____ 9. University College's two Old English <u>professors</u> <u>is</u> the only ones in this part of the province.

_____ 10. Among the crowd <u>was</u> three <u>pickpockets.</u>

_____ 11. Neither the <u>ring</u> nor the <u>watch</u> <u>were stolen.</u>

_____ 12. There <u>are</u> a little <u>group</u> of houses at the curve in the road.

_____ 13. The <u>pieces</u> of the grandfather clock <u>was spread</u> over the floor.

_____ 14. Three <u>kinds</u> of film <u>is</u> sold at the shop.

_____ 15. When <u>are</u> the committee <u>members</u> to meet?

_____ 16. If the <u>audience</u> <u>fails</u> to applaud, the play will close.

_____ 17. Either the <u>motorcycle</u> or the <u>car</u> <u>is</u> to remain uninsured.

_____ 18. The first <u>thing</u> that I saw at the festival <u>were</u> the cheerful faces of the crowd.

_____ 19. <u>One</u> of the students <u>who</u> <u>rides</u> to school with me <u>falls</u> asleep each morning in class.

_____ 20. Neither the <u>books</u> nor the <u>record</u> <u>are</u> his.

_____ 21. The <u>number</u> of students <u>who</u> <u>favour</u> the new dean <u>are</u> not large.

_____ 22. <u>Some</u> of the statistics released by the province <u>shows</u> that Vancouver <u>has</u> a high rate of murder.

_____ 23. <u>He</u> <u>is</u> one of the many students <u>who</u> <u>plays</u> basketball well.

_____ 24. The <u>style</u> of clothes that my <u>roommates</u> <u>wear</u> <u>are</u> now very popular.

_____ 25. The <u>similarity</u> in their clothes <u>is</u> just one of those things <u>that</u> <u>make</u> my roommates seem like one person.

_____ 26. <u>All</u> of our exported wheat <u>is</u> not enough for all of the people <u>who</u> <u>is</u> starving.

_____ 27. The top two <u>teams</u> in each division <u>gets</u> to go to the play-offs.

_____ 28. The <u>family</u> <u>eat</u> together every evening.

_____ 29. Neither the <u>sofa</u> nor the <u>chairs</u> <u>needs</u> recovering.

_____ 30. Only <u>one</u> of the houses <u>that</u> <u>were sold</u> has a garage.

Name _____ Date _____

EXERCISE 8-2

Rewriting Subjects and Verbs *8a (p. 237)*

Rewrite each of the following sentences, changing the italicized words in the first group from singular to plural and those in the second group from plural to singular. Underline these changes. Make all other necessary changes. Check your work by reading your rewritten sentences aloud.

> *Example:* A good *grade* was her only goal.
>
> *Good grades were her only goal.*

Singular to plural

1. A *star* is a giant *ball* of glowing gas.

2. A *star* shines both day and night, even though *it* is visible only at night.

3. A *meteor* looks like a falling *star* but is really a *piece* of rock or metal.

4. A *double star* consists of a *pair* of stars.

5. A *quasar* sends out strong radio waves.

6. The *life* of a *star* is billions of years.

7. An *astronomer* gets information about the *life* of a *star* by studying star clusters.

8. After a *star* begins to shine, *it* starts to change slowly.

9. The *speed* of this process depends on the mass of the *star.*

10. A *photometer* measures the brightness of a *star.*

Plural to singular

1. *Sounds* are caused by vibrations travelling through the air.

2. Sound *vibrations* travel in waves.

3. *Animals* hear sounds that *humans* do not hear.

4. *Pitches* affect the loudness of a sound.

5. *Echoes* are produced by sound waves striking reflecting *surfaces.*

6. *Bats* make high-pitched *sounds* as *they* fly in the dark.

7. *Microphones* change sound waves into electric currents.

8. Human *ears* hear sounds with frequencies ranging from 20 to 20 000 vibrations a second.

9. The highest *tones* on a piano have a frequency of about 4000 vibrations a second.

10. *Sounds* travel faster through dense *substances* than through less dense *ones.*

EXERCISE 8-3

Review of Subject-Verb Agreement 8a (p. 237)

exer
8

Some of the sentences in the following passage have errors in subject-verb agreement. Draw a line through each faulty verb and write the correct form above it.

reflect

Example: The emblems of a country sometimes ~~reflects~~ the growth and development of the ideas of the founding nations.

1   One of the most important emblems of Canada today are the red maple leaf. This stylized leaf sit as the centrepiece of the Canadian flag, proclaimed as the national flag on February 15, 1965. Before 1965, Canada did not has an official flag. The first flag that were flown were the fleur-de-lis, the royal banner of France. After 1760, two flags was flown, the Union Jack and the Canadian Red Ensign. The Red Ensign were the flag of the British merchant marine and were first authorized for use, with the addition a Canadian shield, on vessels registered in Canada in 1892. In 1924, the Canadian government sanctioned its use on government buildings abroad.

2   The red maple leaf of the flag pick up the national colours, red and white, derived in part from the Red Ensign, but proclaimed with the official armorial bearings, or crest and shield, by

124

King George V in 1921. The single, stylized maple leaf also echo the three maple leaves from the crest and shield. This sprig of three leaves symbolize a new nation of many peoples. The sprig are underneath the four quarters which displays the arms of England, Scotland, Ireland, and France, Canada's founding nations. Interestingly, these three leaves was originally green, but in 1957, they was changed to red, and the double connection with the proclamations of 1921 were strengthened.

3   The change from green to red leaves brought the crest and shield into accord with Canada's national and hereditary colours and furnish a reminder of the vivid autumnal reds of a Canadian fall. Two red strips borders the flag, echoing the red of the maple leaf which sit at its centre, and they not only forms another link back to the crest and shield, but also creates a visual representation of Canada's official motto, "From sea to sea."

EXERCISE 8-4

Pronouns and Antecedents   *8b (p. 245)*

Draw an arrow to the antecedent of each italicized pronoun in the following sentences. If the pronoun agrees with its antecedent, mark the sentence *C* on the line to the left. If the pronoun does not agree with its antecedent, cross out the pronoun and write the correct form on the line.

Example: ____*his*____ Neither Tom nor Bud enjoyed ~~their~~ vacation.

_____ 1. No one can know if *they* will get a job in June.

_____ 2. The growing complexity of economics has not lessened *their* appeal to students.

_____ 3. The teachers' union lost *their* right to bargain.

_____ 4. Anyone who turned in a late paper had *their* grade reduced.

_____ 5. Does everybody know where *they're* going now?

_____ 6. Neither Herbert nor his brothers could find *their* book bags.

_____ 7. An elephant never eats leaves or bark that has fungus growing on *them*.

_____ 8. Bettors tend to follow *his or her* own whims at the racetrack.

_____ 9. Every dog on the block barked *themselves* hoarse that night.

126

_____ 10. The College of Arts and Sciences changed *their* entrance requirements.

_____ 11. Neither of the two cars is known for *their* fuel economy.

_____ 12. Every police officer anticipated the danger *they* would encounter.

_____ 13. The manager or the employees will get *their* raises, but not both.

_____ 14. No one could see where *they* were going because of the fog.

_____ 15. Each of the employees got a raise on *his or her* anniversary with the company.

_____ 16. Someone had left *his* shoes in my locker.

_____ 17. Either Ms. Orosco or Ms. Olsen will receive an award for *her* teaching.

_____ 18. If a person has no pride in *their* appearance, others can always tell.

_____ 19. None of the engineers bidding on the contract thought *his* bid would be too high.

_____ 20. Families should install at least one smoke alarm in *their* homes.

EXERCISE 8-5

Agreement: Review   *8a-b (pp. 237-251)*

Rewrite the following passage, changing each occurrence of *person* to *people*. Change corresponding verbs and pronouns, together with other related words as necessary. Underline all changes as you make them.

> *Example:*   (sentence 2)
>
> *One side says that terminally ill <u>people</u> should be allowed to die without having <u>their lives</u> extended with special treatments and equipment.*

An argument new to our modern age is that of the right to die. One side says that a terminally ill person should be allowed to die without having his or her life extended with special treatments and equipment. The other side says that a dying person should be kept alive by his or her doctor for as long as possible. In earlier days, before the advent of modern technology, a terminally ill person simply died in his or her bed. Now that life can be extended for weeks and months in a period of protracted dying, we have the problem of how much a person should have to say about his or her own death.

In many countries, it is legal for a person who believes strongly in his or her right to die to draw up a "living will." With this document, a person can direct physicians not to extend his or her life by artificial means—that is, not to use any treatment whose sole purpose is to put off an inevitable death. A person draws up this living will while he or she is still in good health and of sound mind. And in the countries where these documents are legal, physicians will abide by them.

There is still some opposition to such a practice, however. A person should be kept alive, so goes the argument, to leave the way open for a miraculous recovery or a new treatment or cure. The next step after allowing a person to die is to take that person's life in order to shorten his or her pain and suffering. Called *euthanasia* or *mercy killing,* this practice is less widely accepted than that of writing living wills, although there are many who say that a terminally ill, suffering person should be assisted in his or her death. The problem is a difficult one that has no easy solution.

Chapter 9   Adjectives and Adverbs

EXERCISE 9-1

Identifying Adjectives and Adverbs   *9a-d (pp. 252-255)*

In each sentence, circle the appropriate form from the pairs in parentheses. Identify the circled modifiers as adjectives *(adj)* or adverbs *(adv)* on the lines to the left.

Example: *adv* Skating has become a *(real,* (*really*)) popular sport.

_____ 1. A sport that has grown *(fast, fastly)* in popularity is in-line skating.

_____ 2. In-line skates *(can't hardly, can hardly)* be compared to traditional roller skates.

_____ 3. They are *(more, most)* like ice skates.

_____ 4. These *(most unique, unique)* new skates have all four wheels in a row.

_____ 5. They were invented to keep hockey players in *(better, more better)* shape off season.

_____ 6. In-line skates are *(faster, more faster)* than traditional roller skates.

_____ 7. They also are *(most, more)* maneuverable.

_____ 8. Consequently, many skaters view in-line skates *(approvingly, approving)*.

_____ 9. Skaters like the excitement they get from skating *(rapidly, rapid)* downhill.

_____ 10. Of course, these skates are *(more expensiver, more expensive)* than traditional roller skates too.

_____ 11. At $400, some of these skates are *(almost, most)* too expensive for many people.

_____ 12. Some of the skates, however, are not *(nearly, near)* so costly.

_____ 13. In-line roller skates were made *(first, firstly)* in the United States.

_____ 14. They are popular in Canada too; however, the market is (smaller, smallest).

_____ 15. Of the two kinds of roller skates, in-line and traditional, thrill-seekers consider the newer model *(more attractively, more attractive)*.

EXERCISE 9-2

Correcting Adjectives and Adverbs   *9a-h (pp. 252-260)*

In each sentence below, identify any incorrect form of a modifier by crossing it out and inserting the correct form on the line to the left. If the adjectives and adverbs are correct as given, write *C* on the line.

> *Example:*   *worst* July is the ~~worse~~ time to visit the Southwestern deserts.

_____ 1. They never complained of being real lonely.

_____ 2. A special designed mirror enabled him to drive.

_____ 3. We tourists located the hotel easy.

_____ 4. Doesn't nobody know how to repair this clock?

_____ 5. Greg is surely going to lose his job.

_____ 6. It was so foggy that we couldn't hardly see the road.

_____ 7. Playing bad for one game was no reason to give up.

_____ 8. Keith was one of the most brightest students to graduate from this school.

_____ 9. The bus driver applied the brakes quick to avoid hitting the bicyclist.

_____ 10. Don't never speak bluntly to the dean of students.

_____ 11. Beating the Hartford tennis team is near impossible.

_____ 12. Of the two athletes, Reggie has the highest average.

_____ 13. How sudden did he stop?

_____ 14. Harry always takes arguments serious.

_____ 15. San Francisco's transportation system remains most unique.

_____ 16. My foot hurt so bad that I could not walk.

_____ 17. Oliver executed the pass play perfectly.

_____ 18. A person should always drive safe.

EXERCISE 9-3

Using Articles Appropriately   9i (p. 260)

Insert *a, an,* or *the* as appropriate in the blank spaces, or leave the space blank if an article is not needed.

> *Example:* Many students rent _____ apartments while they are
> in _____ school. [no articles]

1. Renting _____ apartment can be less stressful if you observe _____ few tips.

2. First, try to view _____ apartment you have in mind rather than _____ similar one.

3. Make sure _____ apartment is big enough for you, your room-mates, and all of your belongings.

4. Plan to pay no more for _____ rent than 30 percent of your income.

5. Request _____ written lease and read it carefully.

6. Do not sign _____ lease until you understand it.

7. Ask for _____ check-in sheet to list damage in _____ apart-ment before you move in.

8. Make _____ copy of _____ list for your record.

9. Find out what _____ policy is for vacating _____ apartment.

10. If _____ policy requires _____ month's notice, you could pay extra _____ for late notice.

11. Invest in _____ renter's insurance; _____ cost is minimal and could be worthwhile.

12. Know _____ person you should contact for _____ repairs.

13. When you move, leave _____ forwarding address with _____ apartment owner.

14. Ask for _____ receipt when you turn in _____ keys.

Part III CLEAR SENTENCES

Chapter 10 Sentence Fragments

EXERCISE 10-1

Revising Sentence Fragments I   *10a-e (pp. 258-265)*

Some of the following items are sentence fragments. Rewrite each fragment by expanding it to a complete sentence or connecting it to a complete sentence. If the word group is a complete sentence, write *C* to the left of it.

> *Example*:   A common cause of death and property loss.
>
> *Home fires are a common cause of death and property loss.*

1. Many homes do not have fire extinguishers.

2. Devices for putting out small fires, such as those started in waste-baskets or mattresses.

3. A fire extinguisher, in addition to a smoke detector.

4. Both devices can protect a home from the hazards of fire.

5. Because every day fires break out in 200 homes in Canada.

6. Every home should have at least one fire extinguisher.

7. Preferably several, and the homeowner or renter should know how to operate each extinguisher.

8. Rated by a system of numbers and letters.

9. Higher numbers indicating an extinguisher capable of putting out larger fires.

10. Such as 9B having a greater capacity than 3B.

11. And 2A having a greater capacity than 1A.

12. The A rating refers to fires that burn ordinary materials.

13. B refers to flammable liquid fires.

14. C to fires in electrical equipment.

15. Safety experts recommend extinguishers with a 1A:10BC rating for fire safety in homes.

16. A BC-rated extinguisher for boats and cars.

17. Because there the danger is greater for electrical and flammable liquid fires.

18. If a fire breaks out in a home, a person should first get everyone out of the house.

19. And then use the extinguisher to try to put out the blaze.

20. Directing the nozzle from side to side.

21. To call the fire department.

22. If the fire doesn't go out immediately.

Name _____ Date _____

EXERCISE 10-2

Revising Sentence Fragments II   *10a-e (pp. 258-265)*

Most of the following passages contain a sentence fragment. Identify each fragment by writing the number preceding it on the line to the left. Then rewrite the passage to correct each fragment, adding the fragment to a complete sentence in the passage or changing the fragment to make it a complete sentence. If there is no fragment in the passage, write *C* on the line.

Example: ___*2*___ [1]After graduating from secondary school, I decided to take a year off before going to University. [2]To work and study in Europe.

My plan was to work and study in Europe.

_____ 1. [1]Getting a job that would allow me to earn some money and improve my language skills. [2]This first step proved to be the easiest.

_____ 2. [1]A French Immersion teacher recommended me for a position as an au pair with a family in Paris. [2]Looking after three children.

_____ 3. [1]In order to be an au pair, I had to have graduated from secondary school. [2]Nevertheless, registering in a language program at an accredited school. [3]At an appropriate level.

_____ 4. [1]Au pairs are protected by French law. [2]That protection, however, comes with a bureaucratic price. [3]The documents needed for the special visa, including that school registration, are many.

_____ 5. [1]According to the French consulate in Toronto, originals and two photocopies of seven other documents. [2]Most were relatively easy to obtain.

_____ 6. [1]The most difficult one to obtain was the *Accord de placement Au Pair.* [2]Obtained from the local employment office in Paris before the consulate in Toronto would consider a visa application.

_____ 7. [1]However, if you are not yet eighteen, in order to get that form approved in France, you need notarized parental approval. [2]On a special form from Paris.

_____ 8. [1]The documents travel to and from Paris by diplomatic pouch. [2]Which takes four to six weeks each time. [3]If the correct ones are sent to the correct place.

_____ 9. [1]Making delays and confusion almost inevitable. [2]The "red tape" is frustrating. [3]Complicating and slowing the process.

_____ 10. [1]Once the visa is issued, and work has begun, however, the au pair is protected against exploitation by strict guidelines about working hours, living conditions, payment and time off. [2]Making the whole process, even if difficult, worthwhile.

EXERCISE 10-3

Revising Sentence Fragments III   *10a-e (pp. 258-265)*

The following passages are of the type you might find in advertising copy. Rewrite any sentence fragments as complete sentences, combining them with main clauses or adding words where necessary. If there is no fragment, write *C* in the left margin.

> *Example:* He had a dream of earning a college degree. A dream that all but died.
>
> *He had a dream of earning a college degree, a dream that all but died.*

1. The name of the game is knowing the right people. Because they'll help you invest your money in the right bank.

2. There are two reasons why you should buy Wheatgerms Cereal. It's good for you. And it tastes great.

3. It's the last word in photocopiers. And the very best of its kind.

4. The whole system is state of the art. And we've made it even better.

5. Come in today. See the difference.

6. It's the best pen you'll ever buy. Which is why you should try one today.

7. Gold-plated. Roller-ball tip. For men and women.

8. Luxury. Beauty. Performance. See your dealer today.

9. Wholefarm Bacon. Because there is no better bacon.

10. Toughguy Mowers. Dependability and efficiency worth the price.

11. See British Columbia. Write now.

12. Free. Latest catalogue. Call now.

13. Seeing the best. Buying what you see.

14. Free for the asking. Send today.

15. Looking for good music?

16. One of the most nutritious foods. Raisins. Sweet and good.

17. Think cheese. Made with real milk.

18. Northcountry frozen potatoes. The taste is in the bag.

19. When all you want to do is stop the pain.

20. Announcing the beginning of a new age.

EXERCISE 10-4

Sentence Fragments: Review   *10a-e (pp. 255-261)*

In each passage below, circle the number preceding any word group that is a sentence fragment. Then revise each fragment by linking it to a main clause or by rewriting it as a main clause.

A.   ¹The Great Barrier Reef, stretching for 1200 miles along Australia's northeastern coast. ²Sometimes called the world's largest living thing. ³The reef is made up of living coral. ⁴Purple, green, and pink animals called marine polyps. ⁵More than three hundred kinds of coral have been identified. ⁶Each having a scientific name as well as a common name describing its shape. ⁷For example, mushroom or needle.

⁸In addition to the coral in the Great Barrier Reef, the surrounding sea carries an abundance of other exotic sea life. ⁹Parrot fish, butterfly fish, sea anemones, and giant clams. ¹⁰Unfortunately, the snorkelled tourist swimming off the sandy beaches may encounter a deadly jellyfish known as the sea wasp. ¹¹Of which there are many. ¹²Or sharks around the reef. ¹³But the sharks, it is said, have never attacked. ¹⁴And with a little care swimmers can avoid the jellyfish. ¹⁵A tour aboard a glass-bottomed cruise boat, including supervised snorkelling in the warm waters around the reef. ¹⁶A safe, exhilarating experience. ¹⁷Even for a stranger to the waters.

¹⁸People from North America wanting to visit the Great Barrier Reef should travel to Australia during the northern winter months. ¹⁹If they want to experience Australia's summer. ²⁰Landing in Sydney, they would need to travel north to Cairns. ²¹The nearest city to the Great Barrier Reef.

B.   ¹In the African nation of Dahomey. ²A man's wives were put to death at his funeral. ³Their spirits being supposed to keep him company in the afterlife. ⁴When a king died, many attendants and wives were put to death. ⁵The people believed that a dead person had desires and emotions. ⁶Such as anger. ⁷The dead person could take revenge on the living if his desires were not satisfied. ⁸Thus, a king remained very powerful even after death. ⁹With as much power as he had had when he was alive. ¹⁰Since the dead were so powerful, the survivors had to prevent the dead from becoming envious. ¹¹As well as angry. ¹²So the survivors often sacrificed possessions. ¹³Along with attendants and wives. ¹⁴Appropriate possessions for sacrifice being cattle, food, and jewellery. ¹⁵Such sacrifices guaranteeing continual poverty for the people. ¹⁶War frequently resulted. ¹⁷Because through war the people renewed their wealth. ¹⁸The additional result, however, was the destruction of even more lives. ¹⁹Only in this century did these mourning sacrifices disappear. ²⁰And now the people seem to live in a state of spiritual uneasiness.

exer
10

Chapter 11 *Comma Splices and Fused Sentences*

EXERCISE 11-1

Revising Comma Splices and Fused Sentences
11a-c (pp. 268-274)

Most of the following items are either comma splices or fused sentences. Correct each error in one of five ways: (1) by inserting a coordinating conjunction or both a comma and a coordinating conjunction; (2) by forming separate sentences; (3) by using a semicolon; (4) by reducing one of the main clauses to a subordinate clause; or (5) by reducing one of the main clauses to a phrase. If an item contains no error, write *C* to the left of it.

                                                affecting

    Example: Pollution from smoking is a major cause of illness, ~~it affects~~ smoker and nonsmoker alike.

1. Evidence continues to mount it shows that passive smoke causes diseases.

2. Nonsmokers can be victims of cancer, heart disease, and respiratory illnesses that are caused by smoke in the air they breathe.

3. Parents who smoke in the home are putting their children at risk, roommates endanger nonsmoking partners.

4. Passive smoke is smoke exhaled by the smoker, it is also the smoke emitted from the end of a cigarette.

146

5. Most of the smoke in a room has not been exhaled by a smoker, it has come from the end of a burning cigarette.

6. A smoker inhales, his or her lungs remove some of the tar, nicotine, and harmful gases.

7. The smoke from the end of a cigarette is more hazardous, none of the chemicals have been removed.

8. Some of the more dangerous components of smoke are acetylene, benzene, formaldehyde, hydrogen cyanide, nicotine, and propane, they readily enter the bloodstream of smoker and nonsmoker alike.

9. Setting aside a section of a room to separate smokers from non-smokers is not adequate protection for nonsmokers, the smoke still circulates in the air.

10. The only way to protect nonsmokers from the harmful effects of smoke is to ban all indoor smoking, public buildings and work-places must have restrictions.

Name _____ Date _____

EXERCISE 11-2

Avoiding Comma Splices and Fused
Sentences
11a-c (pp. 268-274)

The following pairs of sentences are correct as written. Revise each pair in two ways, as specified.

    Example: The wedding gifts had to be returned. The wax grapes were no loss.

        Use comma and coordinating conjunction.

        The wedding gifts had to be returned, but the wax grapes were no loss.

        Use semicolon and conjunctive adverb.

        The wedding gifts had to be returned; however, the wax grapes were no loss.

1. The factory once employed five hundred persons. Now there is a parking lot in its place.

   Use comma and coordinating conjunction.

   Use semicolon and conjunctive adverb.

2. She moved to Windsor. However, she found the summers too sultry.

   Use semicolon.

   Use semicolon and move however *to end of sentence.*

3. Leonard Cohen has suffered many bouts of clinical depression. He became a famous poet and songwriter.

   Use a compound predicate.

   Use relative pronoun.

4. Since the release of "Snowbird" in 1970, Anne Murray has been the most recognizable Canadian singer in the United States. She has won several Grammy Awards.

   Use a compound predicate.

   Use semicolon.

5. The airline gave a discount on the Calgary flight. The number of passengers continued to decline.

   Use semicolon and conjunctive adverb.

   Use subordinating conjunction.

6. The band was formed in 1971. Its first hit came the same year.

   Use subordinate phrase.

   Use semicolon.

7. Some vitamins may reduce the risk of certain diseases. In high doses the vitamins are toxic.

Use coordinating conjunction.

Use subordinating conjunction.

8. In the morning there was a rumour that the president of the company had suffered a heart attack. By noon stock prices had dropped sharply.

Use semicolon.

Use comma and coordinating conjunction.

9. Okinawa is a silent survivor of World War II. It lost a third of its population in the U.S.-Japanese battle for the island.

Use semicolon.

Use relative pronoun.

10. The movie got mostly positive reviews. Some critics found the acting unconvincing.

Use comma and coordinating conjunction.

Use subordinating conjunction.

EXERCISE 11-3

Understanding Comma Splices and
Fused Sentences   *11a-c (pp. 268-274)*

Each of the following sentences is a compound sentence with correct punctuation between two main clauses. Write a sentence patterned after each sentence.

exer

11

> *Example:* Deficiency diseases result from a diet lacking certain elements; for example, a lack of vitamin A results in night blindness.
>
> *Our library has several features to help the new students; for example, a librarian is always seated at the information desk.*

1. The official language of Djibouti, a small country in eastern Africa, is Arabic, but most of the people speak Afar or Somali.

2. The bottle-nosed dolphin has a keen sense of hearing, good eyesight, and an excellent sense of taste; however, it has no sense of smell.

3. A dormouse is about three inches long; its tail is another three inches.

4. Werewolves exist in stories of the supernatural; according to legend, they are people who somehow change into threatening wolves.

5. The ancient Egyptians wrote on a paperlike material called papyrus; in fact, they may have been its inventors.

6. Officially Japanese Canadians were interned after the bombing of Pearl Harbor for national security reasons, and for their own protection from mobs; however, senior military and police officers stated that Japanese Canadians posed no such threat, and, in fact, only 150 pieces of anti-Japanese material were ever received.

7. One week after the Normandy invasion, Hitler sent the first V-1 rockets over London; the British called them "buzz bombs."

8. Yams look very much like another root vegetable, the sweet potato, and many people mistakenly confuse the two.

9. The large country in Africa's midsection is called Zaire; however, until its independence in 1971 it was known as the Belgian Congo.

10. Approximately 97 percent of the earth's water is in the oceans, and an additional 2 percent is in glaciers and icecaps.

EXERCISE 11-4

Comma Splices and Fused Sentences:
Review   *11a-c (pp. 268-274)*

In the following essay, circle the number preceding any sentence that has a comma splice or is a fused sentence. Then revise each faulty sentence in the most appropriate way.

THE COUNTRY "DOWN UNDER"

[1]The landing of 1000 convicts on the shores of what is now Sydney marks what Australians claim was the beginning of their nation, it had been "discovered" by Captain James Cook in 1770. [2]In 1788 the first ship arrived with criminals from British prisons they were settled as Australia's first citizens. [3]Since its rough beginning as a British penal colony, Australia has become a country of unique contrasts.

[4]With a national population of about sixteen million, about one million Australians boast convict ancestry. [5]About 20 percent of the population today is foreign born. [6]Many are Middle Eastern and Asian settlers, they have come because of the nation's liberal immigration policies. [7]The original settlers, the aborigines, are in the minority, numbering about 160 000, they are virtual outcasts in Australia today. [8]The country's population is a study in contrasts and diversity.

[9]The land itself provides the greatest contrasts. [10]Geologists say that the continent split off from what we now call South America and Antarctica about sixty million years ago. [11]Its coasts are fertile, but its inland—the outback—is arid, the northeast is tropical rainforest. [12]Off the northeastern coast is the magnificent natural wonder the Great Barrier Reef, to the south the Great Bight provides marvellous surfing. [13]Distances are vast between some of the cities but even more so between settlers in the outback, people may live as much as two hundred miles apart.

[14]Australia has been known for many years for its characteristic animals. [15]Its koalas, kangaroos, wallabies, and platypuses live nowhere else in the world except in captivity. [16]Kangaroos are the national symbol, every year millions are slaughtered as farmers try to prevent them from destroying crops.

[17]North Americans know about Australia from the *Crocodile Dundee* movies, from the novel and television miniseries *The Thornbirds,* and from comedian Paul Hogan, these and other entertainment media give us a glimpse of the world "down under," we can learn more if we want to Australia is definitely in the news.

Chapter 12 Pronoun Reference

EXERCISE 12-1

Unclear or Remote Antecedents
of Pronouns   *12a-f (pp. 276-282)*

Circle each pronoun in the following sentences. Then revise the sentences so that all pronouns refer clearly to their antecedents.

> *Example:* Bed and breakfast inns offer alternative accommodations to tourists (that) have a range in prices.
>
> *Bed and breakfast inns that have a range in prices offer alternative accommodations to tourists.*

1. After the tail pipe fell off Linda's car, Helen knew she would have to take a bus.

2. The conservationists sent the member of parliament a petition to repeal the laws, and the newspaper published an editorial on them.

3. As long as a group of technocrats made regulations for the students, frustration was going to plague them.

4. When biologists speak with economists about environmental issues, they are not entirely clear.

5. When I saw that the dogs had knocked down two elderly people, I ran toward them.

6. The salesman thought that the commission his partner received would make him look bad.

7. I finally paid the bill for dental work that had been lying around for several months.

8. Solar power promises relief from the energy shortage just as synthetic fuel does, but it would be more practical for northern climates.

9. The misspelling on the placard was unintentional but it was not noticed anyway.

10. Small foreign cars differ from small domestic cars they have a solid feel and good acceleration.

EXERCISE 12-2

Implied or Indefinite Antecedents
of Pronouns   *12a-f (pp. 276-282)*

Circle each pronoun in the following sentences. Then revise the sentences so that all pronouns refer to definite, stated antecedents.

> *Example:*   Television networks show such violent programs that people want to try (it) in real life.
>
> *Television networks show such violent programs that people want to try violence in real life.*

1. After being depressed for two weeks, she decided to get over it and resume her routine.

2. When you lived in the nineteenth century, your feet and your horses were your only private means of transportation.

3. Some toothpastes contain abrasives that whiten teeth. However, it warns on the label that the abrasives may wear down tooth enamel.

4. They say that trouble comes in threes.

5. After discussing the repair for the car, we knew it was time it was taken care of.

6. The exam was scheduled for Tuesday, which was not in my plans.

7. Many people shy away from the word *old* because they think of it as being ugly and withered.

8. The soldiers' orders in the war games left them unclear about where they were supposed to go.

9. The buses need more gasoline to run to distant places. They put on more miles, and they break down more often. This makes people's taxes higher.

10. He saw how expensive the supplies were for the art courses, which made him decide not to take them.

EXERCISE 12-3

Pronoun Reference: Combining
Sentences   *12a-f (pp. 276-282)*

Make a single sentence of each of the following sentence groups, omitting unnecessary words and being careful not to alter meaning. Use pronouns where you can, but avoid faulty pronoun references.

Example: Susan's book bag is better than mine. Susan bought her book bag on sale. Susan paid less for her book bag than I paid for mine.

Susan's book bag is better than mine, but because she bought hers on sale, she paid less for it than I paid for mine.

1. It is only two hundred miles to Sault Ste. Marie. I could drive this distance easily.

2. It rained last night. I left my sleeping bag outside. Now the lining of my sleeping bag is soaking wet.

3. By *streetwise* I mean having common sense. Common sense can't be learned from a book.

4. I admire Gwendolyn Brooks's poetry. So I am choosing Gwendolyn Brooks as the subject of my paper.

5. The weather finally turned warm. We painted the porch. Painting the porch was a big job.

6. Rachel takes violin lessons. Rachel was seven years old when she started. Rachel hopes to become a professional violinist.

7. The children were on the playground. The children were watching the demonstrators move down the street. Suddenly the demonstrators began to run.

8. My supervisor called me in this morning. He said I would get a raise. The news came as a surprise.

9. I wanted to back my car out of the driveway. I had to remove the snow from the driveway.

10. We finally came to an understanding. The understanding was over which book we should read. Coming to the understanding was difficult for all of us.

EXERCISE 12-4

Pronoun Reference: Review   *12a-f (pp. 276-282)*

In the following paragraph, circle any pronoun whose antecedent is unclear, remote, implied, or indefinite. Then revise the sentences as necessary so that all pronouns refer clearly and appropriately to a definite and stated antecedent.

The three-storey building, which had been constructed in 1935, was used for many years as a dormitory. Its wooden stairs were badly worn by the feet of thousands of students. It is a wonder that they never broke while they were hauling their heavy suitcases up to the third floor. Nothing had been repaired in it because it was deemed too costly. Then two years ago the building was turned into offices for the Arts and Sciences faculty. This causes less wear and tear on it. However, no refurbishing has ever been done to them. Recently, though, Professor Pines told Doctor Wiley that because of her efforts some funding might soon be allocated to redecorate them. I hope she is right. That will certainly please many faculty members who have found the rooms depressing.

Chapter 13 Shifts

EXERCISE 13-1

Revising for Consistency   *13a-c (pp. 283-288)*

The sentences below have unnecessary shifts in person, number, tense, mood, subject, voice, or form of quotation, as identified in parentheses. Revise each sentence to achieve consistency.

> *Example:*   The meeting was to be attended by representatives from three colleges, but they could not agree on where to meet. *(subject, voice)*
>
> *Representatives from three colleges were to attend the meeting, but they could not agree on where to meet.*

1. He said he bought the recorder without asking would it work. *(quotation)*

2. A person should stay clear of credit cards because they encourage you to spend more money than you have. *(person)*

3. To have it printed, take it to the shop on Wednesday, and then you should call the next day. *(mood)*

4. Although the poet's words are fascinating, I do not know what they meant. *(tense)*

5. She wanted to buy flannel, but it was learned that she was allergic to flannel. *(voice)*

6. If one wants to get the most from college, you must work hard, ask questions, and keep an open mind. *(person)*

7. The two countries had had peaceful relations for a decade when suddenly a border dispute erupts into a war. *(tense)*

8. A Canadian going to a Japanese bath for the first time should have left his or her modesty at home. *(tense)*

9. He said my face was red and asked was I embarrassed? *(quotation)*

10. When someone receives repeated nuisance phone calls, they have no choice but to change their number. *(number)*

11. After a mugger attacked the elderly woman, she was taken to the hospital by police. *(subject, voice)*

12. To get the dog to swallow the pill, place it in the dog's mouth, and then the dog's throat should be stroked. *(subject, voice, mood)*

13. Everyone should be aware that poor night vision can endanger your life. *(person)*

14. The crowding one experiences at a beach can make you wish you had stayed home. *(person)*

15. The characters in the movie are average people, but they had more than average problems. *(tense)*

EXERCISE 13-2

Shifts: Review   *13a-c (pp. 283-288)*

In the following paragraph, underline any unnecessary or confusing shifts in person, number, tense, mood, subject, voice, or form of quotation. Then revise the paragraph to achieve appropriate consistency both within sentences and from sentence to sentence.

exer
13

Our trip to the beach got off to a bad start when the car has two flat tires two kilometres from home. You can always count on some trouble with our car but usually nothing this annoying. We arrived at the motel late, but fortunately our reservations had not been cancelled by the manager, who remembers us from the last time we vacationed there. He asked how long would we be staying and did we want the seafood special for dinner. We checked into our room, and our luggage was unpacked. Everything was going smoothly. Then we went to dinner and turned in for the night. One would have expected that the rest of the vacation should be routine if not fun. But that night each one of us gets sick from their seafood dinner. The next morning the rain came, and for three days we just sat in the room playing cards until it was time that our trip home could be made.

Chapter 14 Misplaced and Dangling Modifiers

EXERCISE 14-1

Revising Misplaced Modifiers   *14a-g (pp. 289-296)*

In the following sentences, underline each misplaced modifier and then revise the sentence so that the meaning is clear. Write *C* to the left of sentences that are correct.

> *Example:*   A vegetarian lifestyle is easier to maintain today than it was a number of years ago <u>with the accessibility of plant products.</u>
>
> *With the accessibility of plant products, a vegetarian lifestyle is easier to maintain today than it was a number of years ago.*

1. Many people have, as a lifestyle, chosen vegetarianism.

2. They feel that eating all animal flesh is wrong.

3. People who see immorality in eating meat often become vegetarians.

4. Some vegetarians just eat plant products.

5. They limit their diet to grains, legumes, vegetables, fruits, nuts, and seeds for maintaining nutrition and their sense of morality.

6. Others only supplement their diet with dairy products such as cheese and milk.

7. Still others eat, as well as plants and milk products, eggs.

8. It is not necessary, in order to have adequate protein in the diet, to eat meat.

9. Many plant products have high levels of protein such as nuts and legumes.

10. A vegetarian feels that carnivores, if they were to consider the source of their meat, would have less of an appetite for it.

11. Consumers see carcasses hanging in the butcher shop or chickens being slaughtered no longer.

12. Meat comes packaged and ready for cooking today.

13. Vegetarians say that a trip to a slaughterhouse might cure carnivores of their taste for meat some day.

14. Vegetarians also remind meat eaters of the risk of raising cattle to the environment.

15. South American rain forests are destroyed so that more cattle can be raised to supply beef for North American fast-food restaurants at an alarming rate.

EXERCISE 14-2

Placing Adjectives and Adverbs in Order

14f-g (pp. 294-296)

Place the adjectives and adverbs in their correct positions before their nouns.

Example: her *paperback* *history* book *(history, paperback)*

1. the _____ _____ _____ tree *(oak, twisted, old)*

2. some _____ _____ _____ laws *(religious, Hindu, modern)*

3. Aunt Sally's _____ _____ _____ armoire *(Norwegian, enormous, antique)*

4. any _____ _____ _____ typewriter *(functional, electric, moderately)*

5. the _____ _____ newspaper *(daily, week-old)*

6. a _____ _____ _____ sandwich *(ham, hot, thick)*

7. one _____ _____ , _____ _____ banana *(overripe, forgotten, long, disgustingly)*

8. a pair of _____ _____ _____

   _____ shoes *(leather, new, red, patent)*

9. a _____ _____ _____ pen *(felt-tip, black, worn-out)*

10. the _____ _____ _____ car *(fourteen-year-old, yellow, convertible)*

11. some _____ _____ _____ software *(computer, released, recently)*

12. two _____ _____ _____ shirts *(silk, grey, extra-large)*

exer
14

EXERCISE 14-3

Revising Dangling Modifiers   *14h (p. 296)*

14h (p. 296)

Most of the following sentences contain dangling modifiers. Rewrite each incorrect sentence by changing either the phrase or the main clause. When you keep the verbal phrase, make sure that its implied subject (the person or thing performing the action) is the same as the subject of the sentence. If a sentence is already correct, write *C* in the space below it.

exer
14

> *Example:* To operate a citizen's-band radio, the fee is no longer required.
>
> *To operate a citizen's-band radio, one no longer needs to pay a fee.*

1. When reading poetry, rhythm often contributes to meaning.

2. After buying a new pair of boots, they should be treated with a protective finish.

3. To recover from the surgery, the vet recommended that we leave our puppy overnight.

4. When painting the walls, care should be taken to protect the floor from dripping brushes.

5. After adding three cups of ground chickpeas, the pot should be heated.

6. Taking a look at the gifts, the smallest box was the one the child selected.

7. Going for a touchdown, the quarterback lofted the ball.

8. Being a nonconformist, a multicoloured wig was what she chose to wear.

exer
14

9. With no concern that the audience was bored, Carson's lecture continued for two hours.

10. To get the employer's attention, your résumé should be attractive and informative.

11. To get the costumes done in time for tonight's taping, help is needed in the costume department.

12. To avoid overcooking your eggs, a low fire should be used.

13. Having been told the qualifications for jurors and then shown a videotape, it was time for lunch.

14. When entering the building, your identification card should be in clear view.

15. Having broken my ankle, my brother has been driving me to school.

Name _____ Date _____

EXERCISE 14-4

Misplaced and Dangling Modifiers:
Review   *14a-h (pp. 289-296)*

Underline any misplaced or dangling modifiers in the following paragraph. Then revise the paragraph by moving modifiers, adding words, or rewriting sentences as necessary.

To successfully and calmly wait at a dentist's office before having your teeth drilled, a little preparation can make a great difference. First, select for taking along to the dentist's office your own book. Never plan to read old magazines dentists set around their waiting rooms that are always dog-eared, dated, and boring. Such magazines cannot provide you any escape from anticipating the pain that awaits you. Second, because you only by arriving early can increase your anxiety, arrive exactly on time and hope your wait will be brief. Third, have a good joke that you can tell the dentist in mind, because a dentist will be less likely to hurt you who is not feeling tense. By keeping the dentist at ease, the most important step will be achieved. A big pain, however, comes when the dentist finishes. It is then that you must pay the bill.

Chapter 15 Mixed and Incomplete Sentences

EXERCISE 15-1

Revising Mixed Sentences   *15a-b (pp. 301-305)*

Revise each mixed sentence below by changing, adding, or deleting words as needed to make its parts fit together in grammar and meaning.

> *Example:*   The team that won was the result of bad refereeing.
>
> *The team's winning was the result of bad refereeing.*

1. While bargaining for a discount was how she made the clerk angry.

2. Just because you took a course in computer programs doesn't mean you're an expert.

3. Hesitation is when you lose your chance.

4. For someone who knows that fighting and sports are not necessarily related could be very disturbed at a hockey game.

5. The hardware store that burned down on First Street was caused by an arsonist.

6. The reason he was lonely was because he had a quick, violent temper.

7. When you have a college education means that you have more skills for the job market and a better knowledge of the world.

8. By being obedient to the rules of my parents has kept me out of trouble.

9. Psychology is where people study behavioural characteristics.

10. The use of a little mustard in egg salad improves the flavour.

11. If you want to know the time of the meeting, it starts at 6:15.

12. By sending your order now qualifies you for a special gift.

13. Because the bus was late was why I missed class.

14. On the way to the train was when I fell and broke my ankle.

EXERCISE 15-2

Revising Incomplete Sentences   *15c-e (pp. 305-308)*

Adding or changing words as necessary, rewrite the following sentences to provide any omitted words or to complete the compound constructions and comparisons.

> *Example:*   The apartment was as roomy as any other house.
>
> *The apartment was as roomy as any house.*

1. We suspect that Judy is more devoted to music than Andy.

2. The administration claims to believe and plan for the college's future.

3. Some brands of vodka contain more alcohol than any beverage.

4. I was going one hundred and thirty kilometres per hour and stopped for speeding.

5. The Hilton's room service is as good as the Holiday Inn.

6. They were fond and totally devoted to their grandchild.

7. The second-night audience found the play more impressive than the opening-night audience.

8. This sandwich is as good, if not better than, the ones my mother makes.

9. Thank you if you have supported us in the past and in the future.

10. Faulkner's novels are more complex than any author's.

11. The audience saw the musician on the podium was unable to proceed.

12. Fruit juice stains are harder to remove than grass.

13. I came to realize some points in the article are true.

14. All those opposed or in favour of the resolution raised their hands.

EXERCISE 15-3

Mixed and Incomplete Sentences:
Review   *15a-e (pp. 301-308)*

Circle the number preceding any mixed or incomplete sentence in the following paragraph. Then revise the paragraph by changing, deleting, or adding words as necessary.

[1]During the first day at university was somewhat frightening for me. [2]I was unsure of my ability to meet new people and do well in my classes. [3]I began feeling more secure when I met my roommate, who was friendlier than any student I had met so far. [4]The second day I went to my classes and found the professors and my classmates were all human. [5]Most were as nice, or nicer, than I could have expected. [6]When I got my assignments gave me even more security. [7]By making it through the third day relaxed me. [8]I knew my schedule very well and begun to make friends. [9]On the first weekend was when I thought I'd go home. [10]But I'm so at ease now I'll stay on campus.

EXERCISE 15-4

Omissions and Faulty Repetitions   *15e (p. 307)*

Add needed subjects, expletives, or verbs, and delete faulty repetitions of subjects, objects, or other words.

> *Example:*   Mexico City, the capital of Mexico, ~~it~~ was built on the site of the Aztec capital city.

Were two major earthquakes in Mexico City 1985. The two quakes they happened on September 19 and 20. They measured 8.1 and 7.3 on the Richter scale. The powerful earthquakes killed more than 7000 people and damaged thousands buildings. Was a bad time for the people of that city. Afterwards, was rubble all over the city.

Some scientists think the reason for the intensity of the quakes it was the underlying geological formations of the region. Mexico City built on an ancient lake bed and bog, making it shake like Jell-O in an earthquake. Another reason, that the city is near the boundary of two tectonic plates. These tectonic plates, which make up the earth's crust, they collided, and one slipped under the other, causing the quake. The centre of the quake 224 miles from Mexico City.

Was another serious earthquake in Mexico City only 27 years earlier. Was in 1957 that extensive damage occurred. Many of the places that were destroyed they were never rebuilt.

Name _____ Date _____

Part IV EFFECTIVE SENTENCES

Chapter 16 Using Coordination and Subordination

EXERCISE 16-1

Using Coordination   *16a (p. 314)*

Combine each pair of simple sentences into one sentence, using the coordinating conjunction that is most appropriate for meaning. Choose *and, but, or, nor, for, so,* or *yet.*

> *Example:* Many animals, including humans, perceive colours. The ways they see colours may differ.
>
> *Many animals, including humans, perceive colours, but the ways they see colours may differ.*

1. The human eye can distinguish about 10 million colours. We have names for only a few.

2. A friend may tell you that his new car is blue. The blue you imagine may not be the blue of his car.

3. The cells in the eye that distinguish colours function only in light. In dim light we see only tones of grey.

4. The cells that perceive colours are called *cones*. Those that perceive black and white are called *rods*.

5. Rods function better than cones in semidarkness. They are sensitive to movement in dim light.

6. People who are colour-blind may have some nonfunctioning cones. They cannot see particular colours.

7. You can call red, blue, and yellow the primary colours. You might also designate them as red, blue, and green.

8. The eye is quite adept at distinguishing fine differences in colour. Sometimes the eye makes mistakes.

9. After looking at something dark, you see a light image when you look away. After looking at a colour, such as green, you see its opposite, such as red.

10. This type of mistake is called *successive contrast*. It's a normal part of vision.

EXERCISE 16-2

Using Subordination   *16b (p. 317)*

Combine each pair of simple sentences below into one sentence by placing the less important information in a subordinate clause, a phrase, or a single word, as specified in parentheses.

> *Example:* Many Canadians are in favour of restructuring the Canada Pension Plan. The government has not yet set up a formal review process. (*subordinate clause beginning with* although)
>
> *Although many Canadians are in favour of restructuring the Canada Pension Plan, the government has not yet set up a formal review process.*

exer
16

1. His shoulders are slightly stooped. He still looks energetic. (*subordinate clause beginning with* although)

2. Tonight he played his greatest role. It was Lothario. (*single word*)

3. We were nearly at the end of our trip. Then we were stopped by the state police. (*phrase beginning with* nearly)

4. The meeting ended. The hall was again deserted. (*subordinate clause beginning with* after)

5. Sparrows are unwelcome pests. They may eat as much as 6 percent of a grain crop. (*phrase beginning with* unwelcome)

6. She wore jogging shoes. The waiter refused to seat her. (*subordinate clause beginning with* because)

7. The patient was recovering. He was depressed and irritable. (*single word*)

8. He felt embarrassed. He could not get a word out. (*phrase beginning with* feeling)

9. German stereo components are often of high quality. They are usually more expensive than Japanese components. (*subordinate clause beginning with* although)

10. I did not know how to interpret the question. It had four possible answers. (*subordinate clause beginning with* because)

EXERCISE 16-3

Using Coordination and
Subordination   *16a-b (pp. 314-323)*

On separate paper, revise each passage to use both coordination and subordination effectively in establishing relations among ideas and in distinguishing main ideas from less important ones.

1. The surviving Dionne quintuplets recently received compensation from the province of Ontario. They received compensation after a sometimes bitter legal struggle. It was also very public. It involved accusations of mismanagement of a trust fund set up for them. It was set up during the province's guardianship of the quintuplets.

2. A triangle was tattooed on the back of his hand. He got the tattoo when he was sixteen. It was a symbol of the instrument he had played. He had played in a rock band. His instrument had been a brass triangle.

3. The night was black, and the road was slippery, and the car, which ran up an embankment, rolled over twice, an action that caused the occupants to be thrown out, while no one was injured. The car was a total loss.

4. The first Canada Cup tournament was held in 1976. It was arranged to bring national teams from Europe to compete against Canada and the United States. It attempted to capitalize on the popularity of the 1972 Canada-Soviet Hockey Series. Canada won against Czechoslovakia in 1976. It lost to the Soviet Union in 1981. Canada won again in 1984 against Sweden. It won once again in 1987. The win came in an exciting three-game final against the Soviet Union.

5. Robertson Davies was born in 1913. He began his life in a small town, Thamesville, Ontario. Some of his later work was set in small-town Canada. He had a lifelong interest in drama. He participated in many stage productions as a boy. His doctoral thesis was on Shakespeare's boy actors. He acted for a year or so with the Old Vic Repertory Company in England. He married Brenda Matthews. He had known her at Oxford. She was working as stage manager at the theatre. He returned to Canada in 1940. He became literary editor of *Saturday Night*. He later contributed to other literary publications. He later moved to the academic world. He was a professor of literature at the University of Toronto for 21 years. He was a respected academic, an actor, a playwright, an outstanding essayist, and a brilliant novelist. He died in 1995.

Chapter 17 Using Parallelism

EXERCISE 17-1

Using Parallelism   *17a (p. 326)*

Each of the sentences below has parallel elements. For each sentence, underline the parallel elements, circle the coordinating conjunction, and then write a new sentence patterned after the original.

> *Example:*   F. Scott Fitzgerald wrote <u>colourful short stories</u> (and)
> <u>romantic novels.</u>
>
> *Professor Smithson sings tuneful folk songs and operatic arias.*

exer
17

1. The people crowded the main street, pouring from cars, trucks, and buses.

2. The Baptists and the Methodists have similar doctrines.

3. Some patients played checkers, others played cards, and still others played shuffleboard.

4. Her clasped hands, her taut shoulders, and her tense face showed her concern.

5. Cigarette smoking is unhealthy not only for the smokers themselves but also for the nonsmokers around them.

6. I will go out of my way to see an old movie or to watch a puppet show.

7. Peering into the room and pushing against the windows, the children stared eagerly at the Christmas display.

8. His cheerful face—caked, chapped, and hardened—revealed not only the nature of his work but also the strength of his character.

9. Grease spots and tobacco stains made a curious design on his pink tie.

10. In the lawn, in the garden, in the orchard—gypsy moths were everywhere she looked.

EXERCISE 17-2

Parallelism: Combining Sentences   17b (p. 331)

Combine each set of sentences into a single sentence, using parallel structures where appropriate.

> *Example:* English began as a Germanic language. It acquired thousands of words from French. It acquired numerous Latin words. It acquired many words from other languages.
>
> *English began as a German language, then acquired thousands of words from French, numerous words from Latin, and many words from other languages.*

1. The history of English has been divided into three stages. The first stage is Old English. The second stage is Middle English. The third stage is Modern English.

2. Old English ran from about 600 to about 1100. Middle English ran from about 1100 to about 1500. Modern English ran from about 1500 to the present.

3. These dates mean that *Beowulf* was written in the Old English period. They mean that Chaucer wrote *Canterbury Tales* during the Middle English period. They mean that Shakespeare wrote during the Modern period.

4. The Modern period is sometimes divided. The first Modern period is Early Modern, ending in 1700. The second Modern period is Late Modern. It began in 1700 and continues to the present.

5. English has its roots in the language of three Germanic tribes. One of these tribes was the Angles. The second was the Saxons. The third was the Jutes. These tribes are commonly called Anglo-Saxons.

6. Some of the most common words in use today have their origin in Anglo-Saxon. Old English is Anglo-Saxon. One of these words is *the*. Another is *man*. Another is *mother*. Another is *and*.

exer
17

7. Middle English dates from the Norman Conquest of England in 1066. Middle English was strongly influenced by the French-speaking Normans.

8. Thousands of French words entered the English vocabulary during this period. Many of them are among our most common. One example is *beef*. Another is *music*. Another is *nice*. Another is *flower*.

9. Modern English is characterized by changes in pronunciation. *Sea*, for example, once rhymed with *hay*. *Moon*, for example, once rhymed with *loan*.

10. These changes in pronunciation contributed toward apparent inconsistencies in spelling today. The invention of the printing press in 1475 contributed toward apparent inconsistencies in spelling today.

EXERCISE 17-3

Parallelism: Review   *17a-b (pp. 326-333)*

The following text has sentences weakened by faulty parallelism. Underline each occurrence and, in the space above it, correct the fault.

1   Six Nations Reserve, southwest of Brantford, Ontario, has the highest population of the 530 reserves in Canada. The resident population in 1994 was approximately 8400, and the total band membership being approximately 18 000. The Six Nations include the Mohawk, Oneida, Seneca, Cayuga, Onondaga, and the members of the Tuscarora nation, who joined the Iroquois Confederacy in the early 1700s.

2   The Reserve, as it is now constituted, is situated on approximately 45 000 acres of the original 675 000 acres and granting in 1784 by Sir Frederick Haldemand to the Six Nations as a reward for their services during the American Revolution. The 'Haldemand Deed' consisted of land 6 miles wide on either side of the Grand River from its mouth to its source. The original lands of the Five Nations were in what is now upper New York State. Both land on the Mohawk and bordering the Susquehanna Rivers— six million acres in all, were sacrificed as a result of the

alliance between the British and the Five Nations and in the time of the American Revolution.

3   This Reserve, despite having an unemployment rate of 29.5 percent in 1994, also had listed in a local directory 264 businesses. Only a small percentage of these businesses, however, were in primary production, and all of those were agricultural, but a large percentage being service-oriented. The Reserve has, since 1994, been formulating plans to foster a production and manufacturing economy to create employment and capital.

4   Living conditions on the Reserve have been the target of both housing and education programs. Six Nations has developed innovative loan and building programs for housing and has also been fostering and expanding Iroquois language immersion programs. The social service network is extensive, and many programs evolving to sustain the community. Six Nations education has also taken steps forward with the Native University Access Program, begun in 1994 with the participation of a University Consortium. Participating students do their first-year studies on the Reserve and then are going to one of the participating universities.

5   Situated on some of the most fertile and beautifully land in Southern Ontario, the Six Nations Reserve has demonstrated its commitment to reclaiming its heritage and fostered its culture.

Name _____ Date _____

Chapter 18 Emphasizing Main Ideas

EXERCISE 18-1

Revising for Emphasis   *18a-e (pp. 335-343)*

Rewrite each sentence or group of sentences below to emphasize the main idea, following the instructions in parentheses. Make your sentences as concise as possible.

> *Example:*   Sea gulls quarrel frequently over food. They quarrel nois-
> ily. But they are graceful in flight. *(Make one sentence,*
> *putting the main idea at the end of the sentence.)*

> *Though they quarrel frequently and noisily over food, sea gulls are graceful in flight.*

1. The prize will be awarded by the foundation for the first time in fifty years. *(Use the active voice.)*

2. Legal gambling can increase tax revenues. It can increase tourism. It can also increase crime. *(Make two sentences, putting the main idea in a separate sentence.)*

3. The kitchen contains poisons that can kill instantly. It is a room filled with perils. It also contains appliances that can be heated to 500 degrees. *(Make one sentence, putting the main idea at the end.)*

exer
18

193

4. He had only six dollars left for his heart medicine, to buy food for his cat, and for his dinner. *(Use parallelism for series elements and arrange them in order of importance.)*

5. It was the winning point that was scored by Shank. *(Use normal word order and the active voice.)*

6. Carrying its prey in its beak, the hawk swooped upward. The hawk was flapping its wings. *(Make one sentence, putting the main idea at the beginning of the sentence.)*

7. A lock was placed on the warehouse door by the guard, who was afraid of theft. *(Use the active voice and place the main idea at the beginning or end of the sentence.)*

8. Because of the steady downpour, the ball could not be held on to by the players, three players tore ligaments, and the uniforms were ruined by the players. *(Use parallelism for series elements and arrange them in order of importance. Change passive voice to active.)*

9. For three hours the speaker discussed nutrition in a monotonous voice. *(Place the main idea at the beginning of the sentence.)*

10. There is some likelihood this year that raises may be withheld by management. *(Use normal word order and the active voice.)*

EXERCISE 18-2

Combining Sentences for Emphasis   *18a-e (pp. 335-343)*

Combine each group of sentences below into one or two sentences
that emphasize the main idea of the group. Make your sentences effective with an appropriate combination of beginnings and endings, parallelism, arrangement of elements in order of increasing importance,
careful repetition, separation, and the active voice. Be concise.

> *Example:*   She does not own a crystal ball. She does not understand
> sports. She won the baseball pool. A four-leaf clover was
> not found by her.
>
> *She does not own a crystal ball or a four-leaf*
> *clover, and she does not understand sports. Yet*
> *she won the baseball pool.*

1. The largest bank cut its lending rate. The other large banks followed. The experts thought the rates would keep dropping. The
   rates held steady.

2. My telephone does not work during rainstorms. I receive calls for
   wrong numbers. I got twenty-seven calls for an ice-cream shop
   one rainy afternoon. I was trying to study.

3. Summer jobs were hard to find. There was no construction work
   in town. The gas stations were going broke. No businesses were
   hiring.

4. Police officers have to keep their car keys handy. They have to know how to drive at high speed. Police officers need special driving skills and habits. They have to know how to drive with caution. They must always remember to park facing an exit.

5. The old woman had white hair. Her face had many wrinkles. She pulled a revolver and took my wallet. Her blue eyes twinkled. She looked innocent.

6. A visit to a nursing home can be depressing. It does not have to be. Taking time to smile and say hello cheers up the residents. Bringing along a small child cheers up the residents.

7. *Breakout* by Ron LeFlore is an inspiring story. It describes his life in prison. It is my favourite biography. He used his skill at baseball to rejoin society.

8. Twelve head of cattle died in the fire. Gasoline spread across the highway and ignited a field. The tanker truck overturned.

9. The tattered magazine described Leon Spinks. He could have been a champion for several years. He seemed to lose faith in himself.

10. Dachshunds shed very little. They are great pets. They are obedient. Dachshunds are gentle with children.

Chapter 19 Achieving Variety

EXERCISE 19-1

Varying Sentence Beginnings   *19b (p. 348)*

Postpone sentence subjects by rewriting each sentence or pair of sentences as specified in parentheses.

> *Example:* The union remained on strike after the votes were counted. (*Begin with* After.)
>
> *After the votes were counted, the union remained on strike.*

1. Penicillin can cure her disease. She is allergic to penicillin. (*Begin one sentence with a coordinating conjunction or a transitional expression.*)

2. The bamboo basket, which looks frail, is really quite sturdy. (*Begin with* Although.)

3. The speech was priced at one dollar a copy, and not one copy was sold. (*Begin with* Because.)

4. The crane fell five stories to the street and smashed a truck. (*Begin with a participial phrase.*)

5. The party invitations omitted the address. Just a few people came. (*Begin one sentence with a transitional expression.*)

6. He never became a great architect, but he was not obscure. (*Begin with* Even though.)

7. Johnson won the game by sinking a shot from thirty feet. (*Begin with a participial phrase.*)

8. Money for travel is in the budget. (*Begin with* There.)

9. Being a good photographer certainly requires skill. It also requires money. (*Begin one sentence with a transitional expression.*)

10. We were swimming in the pond and we heard a shot from across the meadows. (*Begin with a participial phrase.*)

EXERCISE 19-2

Varying Sentences in Paragraphs   *19a-d (pp. 346-353)*

The following paragraphs lack sentence variety. Rewrite each paragraph to stress main ideas by changing some main clauses into modifiers and by varying sentence lengths and beginnings.

1   Almost everyone is afraid of something. Some people are paralysed by multiple phobias, however. They cannot leave the house for fear of an emotional collapse. Treating such people is a slow process. They have to become comfortable with each feared object or situation. The treatment may occur in a laboratory. It may also occur in natural surroundings. The phobias are eliminated one at a time. The patient can often resume a normal life at the end of treatment.

2   Some business executives are concerned about the quality of education in the public schools. They worry about whether students are learning English, math, science, social studies, and communications. These executives are concerned about the future. They are concerned that they will have to hire illiterate workers. They are concerned that their workers will not be able to keep pace with changes in industry. Workers who cannot read well affect productivity and efficiency. Some businesses offer training classes for their new employees. The businesses teach basic skills, and these skills are grammar, typing, and spelling. The executives are not happy with the present state of affairs. They think that uniform testing may be an answer.

3   Some business leaders recommend uniform testing, and they think it may improve the quality of education. The tests, they say, should be uniform for each province and should be comprehensive and reliable. They would be given to all schoolchildren. The tests would make the schools more accountable to the public, and they would tell taxpayers how well students are learning. Taxpayers support the public schools. Accountability is important. Substantive, informed changes are important too, and many business leaders and educators recognize their significance.

Name _____ Date _____

Part V PUNCTUATION

Chapter 20 End Punctuation

EXERCISE 20-1

Using End Punctuation   *20a-f (pp. 358-363)*

Circle the place in each sentence where punctuation should be added or is used incorrectly. Then write the correct punctuation, along with the adjacent words, on the line to the left. If the sentence is already punctuated correctly, write *C* on the line.

exer
20

Example: *address?" he* "Why must I have an addres(?,")he asked.

_____ 1. She shouted, "Watch out for the dog!!!"

_____ 2. Let's watch the news on CTV tonight.

_____ 3. We discussed the question of where to put the file cabinet?

_____ 4. Carry your dirty dishes to the kitchen!

_____ 5. Did he say "Never?".

_____ 6. The title of the story was "Who Was That Kid."

_____ 7. I wondered whether I should finish the exercise?

_____ 8. Dr Baer allowed a 24-hour extension on the paper.

_____ 9. Whether you like it or not, that's the way it's going to be!

_____ 10. Make sure you have a bright enough light for reading

_____ 11. He asked, "When will the package arrive?".

_____ 12. We wanted to know if Jim was late for work again?

_____ 13. The oak leaves are still falling in January

_____ 14. Norbert asked whether the copies were made yet?

_____ 15. The RCMP investigation is almost over.

_____ 16. "For the last time, get out!".

_____ 17. We wondered who was going to pick up the video-tape?

_____ 18. "Watch out!," yelled the chimney sweep.

_____ 19. Rev Winters visited Jessica's brother in the hospital.

_____ 20. "Why are you late?," she asked.

_____ 21. David Woo recently moved to Whistler, B.C..

_____ 22. For more information you can write C.A.R.E. at its Montreal office.

_____ 23. I wonder how anyone can live in Greenland!

_____ 24. CMA stands for both Canadian Medical Association and Certified Management Accountant.

_____ 25. This coat is the best value for your money!

_____ 26. I'm not sure I'll ever get my BA degree.

_____ 27. "Oh! I wish I had brought my umbrella," exclaimed Clara.

_____ 28. Mrs. Horning is a financial planning consultant.

_____ 29. This class will meet from 7:00 to 10:00 p.m..

_____ 30. Queen's University hoped to beat St Olaf College in the football game.

Chapter 21 The Comma

EXERCISE 21-1

Using Commas Between Main Clauses
and After Introductory Elements   *21a-b (pp. 366-370)*

Add commas where they are required in the following paragraphs. Some sentences may require more than one comma, and some may require none.

> *Example:* By studying common features of languages**,** linguists learn about the history of the languages.

1   Discovering the origin of English is like a detective story. Applying deductive reasoning to available clues linguists have traced its beginnings to a hypothetical language called Indo-European. This language did actually exist but there is no record of it other than in the languages that derived from it. In addition to English among these languages existing today are German, Swedish, French, Greek, and Russian. To discover languages' similar roots linguists traced common words. For example *night* in English is *nacht* in German, *natt* in Swedish, *nuit* in French, *nuktos* in Greek, and *noch* in Russian. Interestingly some of these languages that derive from Indo-European are classified as Romance,

or Latinate and some are Germanic. Still others have other histories.

2   On the basis of the presence or absence of certain words in the related languages linguists speculate that Indo-European existed in Eastern Europe several thousand years before Christ. They found evidence of words for *bear* and *snow* but they discovered no common words for *camel* and *ocean*. Using this evidence they supposed that the language was spoken by an inland people that experienced winter climates.

3   At some point Indo-European split into Eastern and Western branches and these branches then divided again. Like English Swedish derived from a branch of Western Indo-European, the Germanic. Greek and French also derived from a branch of Western Indo-European but Russia's origins are in Eastern Indo-European.

Name _____ Date _____

EXERCISE 21-2

Adding Commas to Sentences with Nonrestrictive Elements, Absolute Phrases, and Phrases of Contrast *21c-e (pp. 370-377)*

Add commas where required in the following sentences. (Some sentences may require more than one comma.) If a sentence is already punctuated correctly, write *C* to the left of it.

> *Example:* The poster, a picture of a singer, cost $4.98.

1. The trial, which lasted for three days ended with a verdict of guilty.
2. No one who is related to a police officer would say police work is easy or safe.
3. The Canadian director who may be most popular now is Adam Egoyan.
4. All the banks I hear, refuse to lend money to students.
5. Two men one of them wearing a ski mask robbed the small grocery store where I work.
6. The woman who called me claimed to work at 23 Sussex Drive.
7. We are after all here to get an education.
8. There are few surprises I thought, in tonight's game.
9. Paul Martin who is Minister of Finance voted against tax reform.
10. Her health failing Sarah called her children around her.
11. The audience becoming impatient the theatre manager asked for a little more time to get the sound system working.
12. My dog whose name is Jasper eats two rawhide bones a day.
13. The tax forms six pages of figures were mailed yesterday.
14. The delay during which the pitcher's arm tightened up lasted an hour.
15. The famous Toronto restaurant Pronto has many imitators.
16. I replied, "Yes I would like to play music professionally."
17. Every morning I drink grapefruit juice which contains vitamins and eat a brownie which tastes good.

exer **21**

205

18. Hypnotism still not allowable in court testimony is a fertile method for developing one's memory.
19. The songs of birds for instance, are more complex than they sound.
20. The music blaring next door I was unable to concentrate on my reading.

EXERCISE 21-3

Using Commas with Nonrestrictive Elements, Absolute Phrases, and Phrases of Contrast

21c-e (pp. 370-377)

Combine each group of sentences according to the directions for the section. Punctuate appropriately.

A. Combine each pair of sentences into a single sentence that contains a nonrestrictive element. Use a variety of nonrestrictive elements.

Example: The CN Tower is futuristic and huge.
The CN Tower is the world's tallest free-standing structure.

The CN Tower, the world's tallest free-standing structure, is futuristic and huge.

1. The CN Tower houses both large observation decks and the world's highest revolving restaurant.
   The CN Tower was built over a three-year period.

2. The Tower is a masterpiece of architecture and engineering.
   The CN Tower cost $52 million to build, and is under the mangement of CN Hotels.

3. The building enhances the Toronto skyline.
   The Tower draws millions of tourists every year.

4. Tourists come from all over the world both to see this structure and to see the view.
   Tourists ride the glass elevators to visit the observation decks.

5. Its elevators are amazing.
   Its elevators are glassed in and rise 342 metres to the skypad.

6. The CN Tower is so big that it makes people feel small.
   It is like other postmodern architecture.

7. The central concrete tower is braced by three wings.
   The three wings form a broad 'Y' bracing the hexagonal concrete tower.

8. The 100-metre steel mast on top of the Tower is an antenna.
   The mast is part of the communication equipment.

9. The building has a sophisticated communications antenna.
   The antenna is used for both broadcast and microwave signals.

10. The wings rise to 330 metres and the tower to 450 metres.
    The mast adds another 100 metres to the height of the Tower, for a total of 553 metres.

B. Combine each pair of sentences into a single sentence that contains an absolute phrase.

Example: The Ganges is the world's holiest river.
Hindu mythology actually calls it God.

The Ganges is the world's holiest river, Hindu mythology actually calling it God.

1. The Ganges is named for the goddess Ganga.
The Indians believe that she frees their souls.

2. The Ganges is heavily polluted.
Upstream industries and urban sewage have dirtied it.

3. Many people come to the river to die.
One of its major pollutants is the ashes and bones of cremated bodies.

4. Its waters carry many diseases.
Thousands of devout Hindus bathe in the Ganges every day.

5. The Indian government's health standards are in conflict with religion.
The Indian government wants to clean up the river.

6. Part of the plan is to build sewers and treatment facilities.
Waste water would be processed there.

7. About 75 percent of Ganges pollution comes from waste water.
The treatment facilities would make a big difference.

8. The government also proposes to build large electric crematories. This move is more controversial than that of waste treatment facilities.

9. The old wooden crematories would be replaced by the new ones. The old crematories' waste and ash greatly pollute the river.

10. The government also proposes to build public laundries. Detergents from people doing their laundry in the river would thus be contained and treated.

C. Combine each of the following pairs of sentences to make a single sentence that contains a phrase of contrast.

Example: It was Plato who wrote *Gorgias.*
It was not Aristotle who wrote *Gorgias.*

It was Plato, not Aristotle, who wrote Gorgias.

1. Aristotle wrote *The Art of Rhetoric.*
Plato did not write *The Art of Rhetoric.*

2. Aristotle describes a rhetoric of persuasion.
He does not describe a rhetoric of exposition.

3. Aristotle felt that rhetoric had noble aims.
He was unlike some politicians today.

4. For Aristotle, rhetoric was a means of uplifting an audience.
It was never a means of insulting them.

5. But rhetoric could be used to evoke negative emotions like anger.
It was not used just to evoke positive ones like honour.

EXERCISE 21-4

Using Commas with Series, Coordinate Adjectives, Dates, Addresses, Long Numbers, and Quotations

21f-h (pp. 377-383)

Place commas in the following sentences wherever they are required. (Some sentences will require more than one comma.) If the sentence is already punctuated correctly, write *C* to the left of it.

> *Example:* Our team played tournaments last year in Canada, Japan, and Australia and lost only in Canada.

1. A high-priced skimpy meal was all that was available.
2. After testing 33 107 subjects, the scientist still thought she needed a bigger sample.
3. "Please, can you help me?" the old woman asked.
4. "I need fifty volunteers, now" the physical education teacher said ominously.
5. The excited angry bull was shot to death after it destroyed the garden.
6. The shop is located at 2110 Avenue Road Toronto Ontario M5W 1E5.
7. Many athletes believe that they are more important vital people than those who come to watch them.
8. The open mine attracted children looking for adventure couples needing privacy and old drunks seeking a place to sleep.
9. The aged exotic dancer gave the arresting police officer a phony address.
10. I bought a CB radio on July 2 1998 and I still have not received the missing warranty from the manufacturer.
11. The area around Sarnia Ontario has some of the most polluted air in the country.
12. The records disappeared from the doctor's office in Kamloops British Columbia yesterday.
13. Seven lonely desperate people come to the neighbourhood centre for counselling every night.

exer
21

14. The lantern has a large very heavy base.
15. The town council designated the area's oldest largest house as a landmark.
16. The evil day of 29 October 1929, when the stock market crashed, marked the beginning of the Great Depression.
17. The office is located at 714 W. King St. Fredericton New Brunswick.
18. The November 17 1944 issue of *Maclean's* carried the submarine story.
19. The team lost its final games by scores of 72-66 72-68 and 72-70.
20. Through the wide-open door I could hear them by turns squabbling laughing and crying.

EXERCISE 21-5

Correcting Misused and
Overused Commas
21j (p. 384)

Circle each misused or overused comma. If a sentence is punctuated correctly, write *C* to the left of it.

> *Example:* Tourists who want to visit the United States, should acquaint themselves with entry requirements before leaving home.

1. Legal residents of Canada can enter the United States, without a passport or visa.
2. Visitors to the United States, who do not have Canadian citizenship, must have a valid passport.
3. Canadian citizens who want to enter the United States, should carry identification.
4. This identification should be, a birth certificate.
5. Landed immigrants should carry their papers with them, or some other proof of their status.
6. People taking pet dogs and cats across the border, must have a certificate showing that the animals have recently been vaccinated against rabies.
7. However, puppies and kittens under three months of age are not restricted.
8. Seeing-eye dogs also, are not required to have certification.
9. People who want to take other kinds of pets with them, such as, turtles and parrots, should check requirements.
10. Visitors to the United States should also know, that there are restrictions on plants.
11. There are also restrictions regarding one's return to Canada.
12. Merchandise over certain limits, is subject to customs duty.
13. Canadian residents who have been in the United States for 48 hours, or less, can bring back $100 worth of merchandise.

exer
21

14. Canadian residents, who have been in the United States for more than 48 hours, may bring up to $400 worth of merchandise back with them.
15. Restricted merchandise such as alcohol and tobacco, has limits.
16. The limits are usually 200 cigarettes and 24 ounces of alcoholic beverages.
17. Canadian Customs, like its U.S. counterparts, has restrictions on transporting plants across the border.
18. Tourists who want to bring plants home with them should ask, what these restrictions are.
19. They could also learn that, "bringing firearms into Canada is illegal."
20. The Canadian Customs Service in Ottawa, Ontario, will answer questions about Canadian customs regulations.

EXERCISE 21-6

Commas: Review   *21a-j (pp. 366-384)*

The following paragraphs contain unneeded commas and omit needed ones. Circle every unneeded comma and insert a comma wherever one is needed.

1. Argentina, the second largest country in South America extends 2300 miles from north to south. It is about one-third the size of the United States not counting Alaska and Hawaii. The land was settled by people from many European countries but, most Argentines are descendants of early Spanish settlers, and Spanish and Italian immigrants. The official language of the nation is Spanish. The Argentine people, most of whom live in the cities are generally better educated than people in other South American countries. About 90 percent can read and write. Some Argentines live in large modern apartment buildings and others live in Spanish-style buildings with adobe walls, tile roofs and wrought-iron grillwork on the windows. The homes of the poorer people, of course are not so grand.

2. Argentina is a major producer of cattle, sheep, wool and grain. On the pampa which is a fertile grassy area covering about

215

a fifth of the country, cowboys called *gauchos,* tend large herds of cattle and farmers raise sheep, hogs and wheat. Farther south, in the windswept region of Patagonia people raise sheep, and pump oil. Because the country has such a wide range of elevation, and distance from the equator, it has a climate, that varies greatly. For example the north has heavy rainfall, the central area has moderate precipitation and parts of Patagonia are desert. Being in the Southern Hemisphere Argentina has seasons just the opposite of those in North America the hottest days occurring in January and February and the coldest in July and August.

3   Since its first settlement in the 1500s, when early explorers hoped to find silver in the land Argentina has found, that its real wealth is in its fertile soil and its lively people.

Chapter 22 The Semicolon

EXERCISE 22-1

Using the Semicolon

22a-e (pp. 390-399)

Cross out misused commas and semicolons in these sentences, replacing them with appropriate punctuation if it is needed. If a sentence is already punctuated correctly, write *C* to the left of it.

> *Example:* Some of the wonderful inventions of the past seem hopelessly outdated; however, the principles on which they were based are often still timely.

1. A 1915 cookbook predicts; "The fireless cooker will become recognized as one of the greatest achievements of the century."

2. "No home should be without one," it said, "every cook should use one."

3. Its primary advantages were that it saved fuel and prevented burning and scorching, it also kept cooking odours from spreading throughout the house.

4. The fireless cooker was little more than an insulated box; working on the principle that wood is a poor conductor of heat.

5. The box had depressions to hold cooking kettles, it was constructed of wood or some other poor conductor of heat.

6. Some fireless cookers had stone disks which could be removed and heated, then they were returned to the cooker for keeping food hot.

7. Several popular books of the time gave instructions on how to make a fireless cooker at home.

exer
22

217

8. To use a fireless cooker, the cook would heat the food on a normal stove; until it was heated thoroughly.

9. Foods that required long, slow, low-temperature cooking were suitable for fireless cooking, foods that required high temperatures were not suitable.

10. Foods such as cornmeal mush would be boiled on the stove for five minutes, then they were placed in the fireless cooker for five to ten hours.

11. If the fireless cooker was properly constructed; the mush would still be hot after ten hours.

12. Some homemade cookers, however, were not adequately insulated; and would allow food to become cool.

13. One of the dangers of fireless cookery is that food might not remain hot enough to prevent the growth of bacteria.

14. If food began to cool, the cook was advised to return it to the fire to reheat it, however, the cook was also advised not to open the cooker to see how the food was getting along.

15. Fireless cookers have gone the way of the dinosaurs; although, we still use some of the principles they were based on.

16. Our heavy cookware holds heat, conserving stove energy, our slow cookers extend cooking time to hours, using a minimum of electricity for heating, and our ovens are surrounded with insulating material, holding heat in.

17. Even though we don't ordinarily want to wait ten hours for our cereal to be cooked; with a fireless cooker we could start it the night before and have it ready when we get out of bed.

18. The fireless cooker could have advantages for the cook who works away from home, you could brown the roast before going to work; and put it in the cooker, dinner would be ready when you got home.

EXERCISE 22-2

The Comma and the Semicolon:
Review   *21, 22 (pp. 366-399)*

In the following paragraphs, insert commas and semicolons wherever they are needed.

1   The Aztec Indians inhabited the area around Mexico City from approximately A.D. 1200 until 1521 when they were conquered by Hernando Cortés. One of the most civilized groups of American Indians they lived in and around their capital city Tenochtitlán which was located at the site of the present Mexico City.

2   Families lived in simple adobe houses with thatched roofs. Some of their common foods were flat corn cakes which they called *tortillas* a drink called *chocolate* which they made out of cacao beans and corn beans tomatoes and chili. The men dressed in breechcloths capes and sandals the women wore skirts and sleeveless blouses.

3   Religion was central to the life of the Aztecs. They had many gods most of which they appeased with human sacrifices. As a consequence warfare was conducted largely for the purpose of

taking prisoners who became objects of sacrifice. During the sacrificial rite the priests would often cut out the victim's heart with a knife made of obsidian. The Aztecs believed that human sacrifices were necessary to keep the sun rising every morning and to have success with the crops and warfare.

4   The Aztecs educated their children in history religious observances crafts and Aztec traditions. Outstanding boys and girls were trained in special schools so that someday they could perform religious duties.

5   Descendants of the Aztecs still live in the area around Mexico City still speaking their ancient language but practising Spanish customs and religion.

Chapter 23 The Apostrophe

_____

EXERCISE 23-1

Forming the Possessive Case   *23a (p. 400)*

_____

Form the possessive case of each noun and pronoun below by adding an apostrophe, adding an apostrophe and an -s, or changing the form as needed. Do not change singular to plural.

    Example: Mike Smith   *Mike Smith's*

1. desks   _____

2. James   _____

3. everyone   _____

4. Ed Knox   _____

5. the Mileses   _____

6. fox   _____

7. community   _____

8. they   _____

9. women   _____

10. no one   _____

**exer
23**

11. who _____

12. St. Louis _____

13. father-in-law _____

14. Terre Haute _____

15. sheep _____

16. you _____

17. the Bahamas _____

18. committee member _____

19. oxen _____

20. *Globe and Mail* _____

EXERCISE 23-2

Using the Apostrophe

23a–d (pp. 400-407)

Edit the following passage for use of apostrophes. Insert apostrophes where they are needed and cross out any that are unnecessary.

1   In my job delivering pizza's, I have learned a lot more about the city than I knew before. I have driven to many unfamiliar neighbourhood's and have come to know many new people. I've also been lost many times, trying to find a house or an apartment or trying to read it's address in the dark—all, of course, while the pizzas grew cold.

2   My first weeks experience was one of the worst. I was delivering a large pepperoni supreme to the Swansons' on 49th Street S.E. I drove right out to 49th Street but couldn't find the Swanson's address. I found out the hard way that 49th Street stop's at the river and that 49th Street S.E. starts somewhere on the other side of the river, with no bridge connecting the two sections. Once I found the right section of the street, I drove to the house with no problem. Their name was on a board out in front: THE SWANSON'S, it said. "Its cold," they told me when they took

the pizza, but they did'nt complain. They said they would warm it in their microwave oven.

3   Another time I had to deliver fifteen pizzas to a large party on the north side of the city. I found the place without any trouble, and the pizzas' were still hot when I got there, but the people who ordered could'nt decide who was going to pay me. The guy said the responsibility was her's because she had decided what kind to get and ordered them. But she said, "No, its his house so he should pay for them." It seem's that she did'nt have enough money to pay for fifteen pizzas'. They finally agreed to split the cost. That made me feel a lot better; I was getting worried about what to say to my boss when I brought all those pizzas' back.

exer
23

4   Now that I know the city well, I'll probably have to quit my job because its taking too much of my time while I'm in school. At first I thought I would be able to reduce my hour's, but my boss does'nt want to hire two people to do the job of one. I wonder where I can find another job that will use the experience Ive gained from my pizza delivering but wont take too much time away from studying for my heavy load of class's.

Chapter 24 Quotation Marks

EXERCISE 24-1

Quotation Marks   *24a-b (pp. 410-411)*

In the following sentences, insert single or double quotation marks as required. Be sure to place the marks correctly in relation to other punctuation marks. If a sentence is already punctuated correctly, write *C* to the left of it.

> *Example:* "How many of you," the instructor asked, "have read the assigned story, 'Araby'?"

1. Did Cohen write Suzanne?

2. The nucleus of a cell is its centre, where its vital work goes on.

3. Did I hear you say, The show is sold out?

4. The committee declared, O Canada would be a more appropriate national anthem than God Save the Queen was.

5. Never take Highway 403 unless you like traffic jams, he stated.

6. African man, writes Mbiti, lives in a religious universe.

7. Dickinson's poem first sets the mood: A quietness distilled,/As twilight long begun.

8. Trudeau stated, I invoked the War Measures Act to preserve the public peace.

exer
24

9. Remember the Alamo! was first used as a battle cry at San Jacinto.

10. Dandruff is the code name that CB operators give to snow.

11. Coleridge was ridiculed for writing I hail thee brother in his poem To a Young Ass.

12. The Congo is a poem that experiments with rhythmic effects.

13. Why did you shout Eureka! as you left? she asked.

14. We spent a whole class discussing the word moral, yet we never agreed on its meaning.

15. The characters in the story are, in the author's words, antiheroes; however, none is realistic.

16. Her article, The Joy of Anguish, was reprinted in six languages.

17. Sotweed is a synonym for tobacco.

18. How many of you know the To be or not to be speech from *Hamlet?* asked the drama coach.

19. He said that the test would be challenging; he should have said that it would be impossible.

20. William Blake's s poem The Fly includes this stanza:

> Am not I
> A fly like thee?
> Or art not thou
> A man like me?

EXERCISE 24-2

Writing Quotations   *24a-g (pp. 410-418)*

In the following essays, use separate paper to rewrite all indirect quotations as direct quotations, revising as necessary and inserting quotation marks as appropriate.

A.

COOLING OFF

1   When I was twelve, I went swimming at St. Ben's College swimming pool with my good friend Paul, who is two years older than I. It was a steamy hot summer day when I suggested to Paul that we go for a dip. Chuckling, he told me that I had read his mind.

2   We left in the early afternoon, cruising down the road on our mud-covered bicycles. As we got to the pool, Paul yelled that the last one in was the biggest loser in the world. Naturally he won because I had to lock up the bikes.

3   Two walls of the indoor pool were enclosed in glass, affording a view of the entire campus and the sunny summer day. After we had been swimming for about an hour, I noticed that the sun was no longer shining. In fact, the sky was turning quite dark. I pointed to the leaden grey clouds moving toward us and asked Paul if he thought we should leave.

4   He exclaimed that we should—after one more dive.

5   As we dressed in the locker room, I told Paul that I was nervous about the weather, because I had never seen it change so quickly. When we pushed open the door, the wind pushed back. Rushing out, we ran toward our bikes, unlocked them, and headed in the direction of home.

6   About halfway home, we began to be hit by small pellets of hail. Paul yelled at me to hurry up, that I was falling behind. With lightning brightening the dark afternoon, thunder crashing around us, and hail bouncing off our chilled bodies, we pedalled furiously, seeing my driveway just ahead. As I turned in to the

exer 24

drive, Paul rode on to his house next door, yelling to me that he would see me later.

7   I dropped my bike on the lawn and dashed into the house, looking for a towel and some dry, warm clothes. I wasn't hot anymore.

B.

BRIGHT FUTURE FOR MEDICINE

1   Late twentieth-century research, powered by technological advance, seems to promise phenomenal changes to the treatment of injury and disease. *Maclean's* magazine's (10 Jan. 2000) cover story "Medicine in 2020" includes four articles on some of these advances. In the first article, author Robert Sheppard imagines a day in the life of ordinary and extraordinary medical treatment (41) for a fictional character he calls "Jeannette T."

2   Sheppard's ordinary heroine is an aging baby boomer who muses first on the new seniors' residences her children have mentioned to her, their rooms equipped with beds equipped with diagnostic tools, and then she concludes that those places are for old folks (41) because she is happy with her current regular video call to the public health nurse, and transmitting her own vital signs from the home-monitoring machine while they talk.(41)

3   This "ordinary" or usual care Sheppard envisions for Jeannette he also imagines supplemented by special jewelry which she details, like a wristwatch that measures her sugar levels through her skin and signals the artificial pump in her pancreas when it needs to supply more insulin. (41) She also mentions the glasses her friend with Alzheimer's wears — with the micro-camera programmed to recognize faces and familiar locales. (41)

4   Bringing Jeannette out of her reverie, Sheppard envisions a knock at the door and police officers bringing the news that Jeannette's son has been seriously injured in an accident in northern Saskatchewan. But, they report, the medical team are flying in a surgical robot from Yellowknife. With a satellite uplink, a surgeon here in Toronto can perform the operation. Would she like to come to Central Hospital for a personal consultation?(41) This part of the scenario, then, is the "extraordinary medical treatment." (41)

5   Jeannette goes to the hospital and Sheppard continues his depiction of the medical treatment of the future with descriptions of disinfectant chambers, (42) super sniffers in elevators and air ducts (which) can detect most air-borne viruses, (42) and smart card access to treatment areas. Jeannette is reassured by the quality of care and settles down to watch tele-surgeons (43) operate on her son from as far away as Germany.

6   This whole story illustrates devices and techniques which are now in developmental stages and could become reality by the year 2020. All of it seems so much like science fiction to us now, but, without doubt, in 1949, so did landing a manned spacecraft on the moon.

exer

24

Chapter 25 Other Punctuation Marks

EXERCISE 25-1

Using the Colon, the Dash, Parentheses, Brackets, the Ellipsis Mark, and the Slash   25a-f (pp. 420-433)

Circle the place in each sentence where punctuation should be added or is used incorrectly, and write the correct punctuation, along with the adjacent words, on the line to the left. When more than one mark would be correct in a sentence, choose the mark that seems most appropriate. If a sentence is already punctuated correctly, write *C* on the line.

Example: *exhibit: the* Adams was fascinated by one thing in the exhibit, the power of steam.

_____ 1. Of the nine provinces surveyed, only one New Brunswick had a low suicide rate.

_____ 2. The ring was priced reasonably, ($200).

_____ 3. "Iamb," "trochee," "spondee" all are terms for poetry analysis.

_____ 4. "The penalty is a $500 fine and or a year in jail," the lawyer said.

_____ 5. There are two basic defences: 1 the zone and 2 the man to man.

_____ 6. A good worker, he lacks only one quality tact.

_____ 7. Environmentalists find that incentives, (such as refunds) increase recycling.

_____ 8. The recipe my aunt's favourite calls for three eels.

_____ 9. The discount on the new car was insignificant only $50.

_____ 10. Two of the contestants (Perry and Hughy are my roommates.

_____ 11. In two lines of the poem, Robinson portrays Richard Cory as "a gentleman from sole to crown,/Clean favored, and imperially slim."

_____ 12. The paper said, "People waved from the poopsite (*sic*) shore."

_____ 13. I got a high grade in only one course; Elementary Education 101.

_____ 14. The kit contained the following items, a flare, a wrench, two screwdrivers, one hammer, and a fan belt.

_____ 15. The life of Ernest Hemingway 1899-1961 was exciting by almost anyone's standards.

_____ 16. His new title [associate fireman] brought no increase in pay.

_____ 17. The hide—(alligator)—could not be imported.

_____ 18. The assignment for Friday was a long one pages 200-290.

_____ 19. The cathedral, built in 1295?, was open to tour groups.

_____ 20. "The province's largest drinking foun- tain" that is what the mayor called the new reservoir.

_____ 21. However, she then said, "Let's not forget how difficult it was to bring this water here and ... how much it means to us."

_____ 22. Among the recruiters were IBM, Olivetti, and TRW.

_____ 23. Tolstoy's *Works* [volumes 2 and 3] was on sale for $7.95.

_____ 24. The course depended on only one assignment ... the term paper.

_____ 25. The teacher, actually, his assistant wrote that my paper was "flabby and point- less."

EXERCISE 25-2

Punctuation: Review of
Chapters 20-25   *20-25 (pp. 358-433)*

In the following passages, insert correct punctuation wherever it is missing.

A.

THREAT TO THE EYES

[1]Sunlight is made up of three kinds of radiation 1 infrared rays which we cannot see 2 visible rays and 3 ultraviolet rays which also are invisible. [2]Especially in the ultraviolet range sunlight is harmful to the eyes. [3]Ultraviolet rays can damage the retina the area in the back of the eye and cause cataracts on the lens. [4]Wavelengths of light rays are measured in nanometres nm or millionths of a metre. [5]Infrared rays are the longest measuring 700 nm and longer and ultraviolet rays are the shortest measuring 400 nm and shorter. [6]The lens absorbs much of the ultraviolet radiation thus protecting the retina however in so doing it becomes a victim growing cloudy and blocking vision.

[7]You can protect your eyes by wearing sunglasses that screen out the ultraviolet rays. [8]To be effective sunglasses should block out at least 95 percent of the radiation. [9]Many lenses have been designed to do exactly this but many others are extremely ineffective. [10]When you are buying sunglasses you can test their effectiveness by putting them on and looking in a mirror while you stand in a bright light. [11]If you can see your eyes through the lenses the glasses will not screen out enough ultraviolet light to protect your eyes.

[12]People who spend much time outside in the sun really owe it to themselves to buy a pair of sunglasses that will shield their eyes.

exer
25

233

B.

PARADISE NEXT DOOR

[1]Belize a small country on the eastern coast of Central America covers less than 9000 square miles. [2]Bordering Mexico on the north and Guatemala on the west and south this little nation has a population of approximately 154 000. [3]The official language is English but Spanish and native Creole dialects are spoken as well. [4]The country which was formerly known as British Honduras achieved independence in 1981. [5]Home to Mayan Indians for centuries Belize was settled in the seventeenth century by pirates slavers and shipwrecked British seamen and was ruled by Great Britain until its independence it still maintains strong ties to the United Kingdom.

[6]While sugar is its primary export Belize is known mainly for diving fishing and swimming. [7]Divers come from all over the world to explore its coral reefs and limestone caves. [8]The reef offshore is 176 miles long exceeded in length only by Australias Great Barrier Reef. [9]Divers also like to explore the Blue Hole a chasm in the Caribbean that is 400 feet deep and 1000 feet wide it has stalactites and beautiful corals.

[10]Both the reef and the Blue Hole can be reached by boat from Belize City. [11]This city once the capital of the country is now a tourist attraction because of its location. [12]Belize City is still the largest city in Belize but it has been replaced as capital by Belmopan which is located fifty miles inland. [13]In this new location the government buildings are more secure from hurricanes.

[14]The tallest structure in the country is the ruins called El Castillo built about 1500 years ago by Mayan Indians. [15]Other Mayan ruins are tucked within thick jungles and give spectacular evidence of the ancient civilization.

[16]A major aspect of the Belize economy is the tourist trade however investors and developers have been attracted to the country too. [17]Its stable government and tropical climate both of which spur tourism have drawn foreign business as well.

Part VI MECHANICS

Chapter 26 Capitals

EXERCISE 26-1

Using Capitals   *26a-f (pp. 436-442)*

Substitute new words for all underlined words in the following sentences.

> *Example:*   The <u>Freedom of Information Act</u> has been costly to implement.
>
> *The <u>Refugee Act of 1980</u> has been costly to implement.*

1. The premier gave a radio talk on <u>Christmas</u>.

2. Edith Farrara, president of <u>Grendel Corporation,</u> makes monsters for a living.

3. Carol titled her painting <u>*All Alone in the Wheat.*</u>

4. John still tells <u>World War II</u> stories on <u>Remembrance Day</u>.

5. The waiter explained, "<u>The</u> soup changes every day."

6. Mike asked <u>Grandmother Collins</u> where she was born and heard a fascinating reply.

7. Heffeltooth is a local leader of the <u>Reform Party.</u>

8. Our family attends the <u>United Church</u> on <u>Main Street.</u>

9. My grandfather always forgets to put in his teeth, and <u>Granny</u> then complains.

10. The anti-<u>Islamic</u> group distributed literature on <u>Friday.</u>

11. In <u>English</u> class yesterday, <u>Professor Cohen</u> was upset because <u>Mia</u> wrote her paper on how to make <u>Jell-O.</u>

12. My friend <u>Joe</u> lives on the east side of the park.

13. Ed was always in favour of having lights at <u>Exhibition Stadium.</u>

14. Both teammates are seniors this spring at <u>Technical High School.</u>

15. The book was titled <u>*How to Deal with Stress.*</u>

16. <u>Canada Post</u> seems to make changes every year.

17. Next semester I want to take <u>Industrial Studies 236.</u>

18. Workers in the <u>Netherlands</u> have more vacation time than workers in <u>Canada.</u>

Chapter 27 Underlining (Italics)

EXERCISE 27-1

Using Underlining (Italics)   *27a-e (pp. 443-446)*

In the following sentences, underline any words that should be underlined (i.e., in italics). If a sentence is already correct, write *C* to the left of it.

> *Example:*   The word <u>emotion</u> pertains to feelings.

1. The tankers were blockaded for a week in the Persian Gulf.

2. TNT was used to demolish the building.

3. The Globe and Mail usually printed conservative views.

4. The yard became overgrown with Swedish ivy.

5. We took a tour of a ship, the Bluenose, for only $2.50.

6. Hamlet contains more violence than does any crime drama on television.

7. The clams were so gritty that we could not eat them.

8. Life magazine is a showcase for photography.

9. Shaw's Man and Superman is more often read than viewed on stage.

10. The Great Wall of China was completed in the third century B.C.

exer
27

11. The strange form was the mem of the Hebrew alphabet.

12. She makes the dots on her i's so large that the page looks like an aerial view of the Charles County Balloon Festival.

13. We read the Bible's first five books and discussed them in class.

14. We had to report on the P. W. Joyce book Old Celtic Romances.

15. Gree is an archaic word meaning "satisfaction."

16. A new journal, Fun with Caries, reprinted an article by Brady Hull, D.D.S.

17. The documentary program W5 continues to be quite profitable for CTV.

18. Miserere is the fiftieth psalm in the Douay Bible.

19. Eijkman won the Nobel Prize for medicine in 1929.

20. The expression c'est la vie never gave me much comfort.

21. The professor published her article in the sociology journal Studies in Poverty.

22. I was surprised to see that Wyeth's Christina's World is not a larger painting.

23. The foxglove belongs to the genus Digitalis.

24. My husband, for instance, repeatedly mispronounces the word asterisk.

25. My twenty-year subscription to Boys' Life, given to me by my uncle, has finally expired.

Chapter 28 Abbreviations

_____

EXERCISE 28-1

Using Abbreviations   *28a-f (pp. 447-451)*

_____

Cross out each abbreviation that is inappropriate and write the correct form above it. If the abbreviation is appropriate, write *C* in the left margin.

> *Street*
> *Example:*   Second ~~St.~~ needs to be repaved.

1. The end of Jan. was the last time Alexi smoked a cigarette.

2. Econ. 145 will not be offered next semester.

3. The assignment for Tues. is to read the first ten pages of Ch. 8.

4. Wm. McDougall will address the campus community on Dec. 14.

5. The address will begin at 10:00 A.M.

6. Dan is considering transferring to the U. of Manitoba.

7. One psychological study suggests that people who are greatly self-involved—e.g., who talk about themselves a great deal—are more likely to have heart disease.

8. Joshua Stern, assoc. prof. of geography, will present the result of his research.

**exer
28**

9. The H. of Commons formally adjourned for Earth Day so members could attend teach-ins in some districts.

10. Our conference will be held this year in Sault Ste. Marie.

11. You can write to the B.C. Tourist Development Off. for winter travel information.

12. Or you can write to Banff, Alta., for information about travel to the Lake Louise area.

13. Roots Research Bureau, Ltd., is one of the companies that offer family histories, ancestry charts, etc., for a price.

14. Three of the twelve special centres are located in Ontario, N.B., and Manitoba.

15. The Count Dracula Society has its main office in Los Angeles, CA.

16. The no. of members exceeds one thousand.

17. Since its discovery in 1981, AIDS has spread to many nations.

18. Bert hopes eventually to get an MA in history.

Chapter 29 Numbers

EXERCISE 29-1

Using Numbers   *29a-c (pp. 452-455)*

Cross out any figure that should be spelled out in most writing, and write the spelled-out number above it. Cross out any spelled-out number that should be written in figures, and write the figures above it. If numbers are used appropriately, write *C* in the left margin.

> *Example:* Noted "Pogo" cartoonist Walt Kelly died in ~~nineteen seventy-three~~.
>
> *1973*

1. The tallest building in Toronto is 553 metres high.

2. The U.N. Security Council adopted the resolution on June 1st.

3. "We need another forty cents for toll," said Alex.

4. Estimates of the death toll ranged from 550 to two thousand.

5. Windsor's tallest building is 250 metres high.

6. Our instructor assigned Chapter Thirteen for tomorrow.

7. The unemployment rate rose to seven percent in June.

8. 7800 athletes participated in the 1984 Olympic Games.

exer
29

9. The pact was signed at exactly 9 o'clock.

10. When the game was called on account of darkness, the score was still 7 to 4.

11. Willard Estey, Supreme Court Justice, served on the Estey Commission for eleven months.

12. On December 29th, 1890, about 200 Native Americans and 29 soldiers died at Wounded Knee, South Dakota.

13. When the Cuban Giants baseball team was organized in 1885, players were paid an average of $15 a week plus expenses.

14. The Han Dynasty ruled China from 202 B.C. to A.D. 220.

15. 1 troy ounce is equivalent to 1.097 avoirdupois ounces.

16. You can write the Canadian Broadcasting Corporation at 250 Front St. W., Toronto, Ontario, M5W 1E6.

17. North Americans' eating habits were changed by a major study linking cholesterol and heart disease, released on the 12th of January, 1984.

18. The value of rice exports was estimated at $178 million.

Chapter 30 Word Division

EEXERCISE 30-1

Dividing Words Correctly   *30a-d (pp. 456-458)*

Many of the following word divisions would be inappropriate in a final paper. Some words should not be divided, and some should be divided differently. If a word should not be divided, write the word on one line to the right. If a word should be divided differently, write the correct division on two lines. Write *C* on the line beside any word that is divided correctly.

Example: good-na-   *good-*

tured   *natured*

1. stew-   _____   7. ach-   _____

   ed   _____   ieve   _____

2. rel-   _____   8. fin-   _____

   igious   _____   ished   _____

3. control-   _____   9. head-hunt- _____

   led   _____   ing   _____

4. curr-   _____   10. gui-   _____

   ent   _____   ding   _____

5. accomp-   _____   11. poe-   _____

   lish   _____   try   _____

6. Marx-   _____   12. car-   _____

   ist-Leninist _____   nival   _____

exer
30

243

13. pan-Afri-   _____
    can   _____

14. swarth-   _____
    y   _____

15. techniq-   _____
    ue   _____

16. usa-   _____
    ges   _____

17. cover-   _____
    ed   _____

18. drag-   _____
    ged   _____

19. self-in-   _____
    flicted   _____

20. res-   _____
    earch   _____

21. lit-   _____
    tle   _____

22. sig-   _____
    ner   _____

23. nutrit-   _____
    ion   _____

24. leng-   _____
    th   _____

25. divis-   _____
    ion   _____

26. litera-   _____
    ture   _____

27. bro-   _____
    ught   _____

28. assig-   _____
    ned   _____

29. rent-   _____
    ed   _____

30. regis-   _____
    ter   _____

Part VII EFFECTIVE WORDS

Chapter 31 Choosing and Using Words

EXERCISE 31-1

Choosing the Appropriate Word   *31a (p. 462)*

Revise the following paragraphs to avoid slang, colloquial language, regional words and expressions, nonstandard language, obsolete or archaic words, neologisms, unnecessarily technical words, euphemisms, and pretentious words. Draw a line through each inappropriate expression and write a better term above it. Consult a dictionary as needed.

1   A Rocky Mountain high—what sort of scene does this location bring up for you? Well, the place that pops into my mind is colourful British Columbia. One town in British Columbia that can get anyone high is Whistler, a metropolis at an elevation of about 3000 metres above sea level. The why and wherefore of my getting such a kick out of Whistler is that I spent two weeks there last summer. The redolence of clean, fresh air, the pulchritude of snow-capped mountains, and the abundance of wildlife can make anyone feel great.

2   To repot a plant into a larger container, employ these directions with consummate care. First obtain the necessary materials: your plant that needs repotting, a more capacious pot, some potting soil, and H_2O. With your hand supporting the plant, slap it out of the pot it has been resident in, making sure you don't disconnect the roots from the stem or petioles. Then stick the plant under some gently running water so you can wash the dirt from the roots. Dump some new potting soil into the larger pot and place the plant in the middle, spreading out the roots. Interject more soil into the pot until it nearly reaches the circumscribed edge. Tamp the soil lightly until it's smooth. Add enough liquidescence to moisturize the soil, and set the plant in a milieu where it can soak up sunlight.

3   I was never so ticked off as I was last week when my klutzie roomie—a real flake—totalled my class notes from Econ. They were sitting right there on the desk when my roomie, who was lip-synching MTV, swung her arm around and knocked her week-old, half-finished can of Diet Pepsi all over the desk, including my Econ. notes. Well, I went absolutely postal. By the time she found something suitable (my new sweats) to wipe up the mess with, the damage was done: the ink had run and was illegible. So what could I do but bomb the test? It was a real bummer.

EXERCISE 31-2

Revising Biased Language   *31a-8 (p. 467)*

Revise the following sentences to eliminate biased language.

> *Example:*   Charlotte Battle was Norman Oates's girl Friday for seventeen years.
>
> *Charlotte Battle was Norman Oates's assistant for seventeen years.*

1. Pastor Olsen and his wife Barbara will be honoured guests at the luncheon.

2. Each student should have his books by the first day of class.

3. The mailman was half an hour late today.

4. Under normal circumstances, wolves do not attack man.

5. Each employee should fill out his time card before the end of the day.

6. That old grandpa driving down the road looks as if he can hardly see over the steering wheel.

exer

31

7. If you have any trouble with the washing machine, just call your service-man.

8. I was stopped at a traffic light when a chick driving a Trans-Am rammed the rear of my car.

9. A nurse is always expected to put duty before her personal interests.

10. Has everybody put his name at the top of his paper?

11. Every policeman in this city is equipped with a bulletproof vest.

12. Fishermen should check the wind forecast before going out in a boat.

13. The divers went deeper than man has ever gone before.

14. Every typist should type as fast as she can without making errors.

15. The old geezer is probably a member of the Reform Party and writes his MP every week.

EXERCISE 31-3

Understanding Denotation   *31b-1 (p. 469)*

Circle the word in parentheses whose established denotation fits the meaning of the sentence. Consult a dictionary as needed.

> *Example:* The presiding judge listened intently but remained (*disinterested,* *uninterested*) in the libel case.

1. The president-elect was ready to *(accept, except)* the offer of support.

2. She was strongly *(affected, effected)* by the offer.

3. "It is not *(everyday, every day)* that your opposition comes to your side," she said.

4. "I take it as a *(complement, compliment)* to my integrity as a candidate," she concluded.

5. The landlord *(implied, inferred)* that we had broken the washing machine.

6. In making his accusation, he made *(allusions, illusions)* to other occurrences that had nothing to do with us.

7. Because it was untrue, his accusation *(aggravated, irritated)* us.

8. We are also upset by the *(amount, number)* of times he has been rude to us.

9. "I hope to be back *(sometime, some time)* soon," said our foreign exchange student as we took her to the airport.

10. "Who knows?" I said. "I *(maybe, may be)* in Spain one day myself."

11. "The time here has gone so much faster *(than, then)* I expected," she said.

12. "I'm *(all ready, already)* planning my next trip."

exer

31

249

13. "And if I'm not careful, I'm *(liable, likely)* to be homesick for your home."

14. Jason was *(anxious, eager)* to start his new job at the car wash.

15. He was really *(conscience, conscious)* of the need to start off well.

16. He was hoping to work *(fewer, less)* hours than he did on his last job.

17. His *(idea, ideal)* in changing jobs was to have more time for study.

18. But he *(preceded, proceeded)* to work more hours so that he could spend more money on his car.

EXERCISE 31-4

Using General and Specific Words,
Abstract and Concrete Words

31b-2 (p. 469)

The paragraphs below contain words that are general or abstract. Revise each italicized word, writing in the space above it a word that is more specific or concrete.

1   The *bird* flew up and landed on the feeder. With its claws attached to the edge, it began *eating seed*. Soon *other birds* came and settled on the feeder. They all *seemed to be enjoying themselves*. I felt so *happy* that I was able to *help* them. As they *ate*, they dropped some seed onto the ground, and *little animals* came and *ate* too.

2   One day when I was *young* I had the *experience* of taking my first boat ride with my entire *class*. As *the teacher* helped us off the bus, everyone was *filled with delight*. In the *water* were boats of all sizes and shapes. We all *got on* a *medium-sized* one and found *seats* for ourselves. I was sitting close to the side of the boat. All of a sudden, a *loud* horn sounded and we began to move. We were all *excited*. As I watched our boat pull away from the shore, it seemed as if the people on shore were *moving* and the boat was standing still. We *moved* farther into the lake, and I stood at the side to look into the water. It was *beautiful*. The lake was a *dark colour*, and

exer

31

251

birds were flying all around. I began *daydreaming,* as if in a trance. Suddenly we were back at the dock, and we were all hurrying off the boat and back onto our bus, heading back to school and home, where we would tell our parents about the *enjoyable expe-rience.*

EXERCISE 31-5

Using Idioms   *31b-3 (p. 475)*

Drawing on the list on page 456 or consulting a dictionary as needed, circle the appropriate preposition in parentheses to complete the idioms in the following sentences.

> *Example:*   After much debate, we finally agreed (*with,* (*on*)) a new policy.

1. I was impatient *(for, with)* the class to end.

2. Differing *(from, with)* each other only over money, the couple nonetheless decided to divorce.

3. The request seemed unreasonable, but she complied *(with, to)* it anyway.

4. Though we were angry *(at, with)* each other, we continued to study together.

5. They had corresponded *(to, with)* the same woman for seven years before they learned the truth.

6. The dangers *(in, for)* someone learning to ski are slight.

7. The officer locked the suspect up and charged him *(for, with)* robbery.

8. College is different *(from, than)* high school in unexpected ways.

9. When the jury acquitted O'Reilly *(for, of)* murder, the townspeople were delighted.

10. During his visit the Pope stayed *(in, at)* Denver only briefly, but he electrified the city.

11. Although rewarded *(by, with)* increasingly flavourful foods, the pigeon would not learn any new tricks.

12. I waited impatiently *(on, for)* his arrival.

exer

31

13. At the age of fourteen, Lucy was independent *(of, from)* her parents.

14. My courses vary *(in, from)* difficulty, so I have no trouble setting my priorities when I study.

15. Some researchers are impatient *(at, with)* the arguments of the theorists.

16. I was preoccupied *(with, by)* my work.

17. The shop charged me *(with, for)* a purchase that I had forgotten.

EXERCISE 31-6

Using Fresh Expressions   *31b-5 (p. 47*

Identify the trite expression or expressions in each sentence below, and revise the sentence to eliminate such expressions.

> *Example:*   She was meek as a lamb, though she was a superb public speaker.
>
> *She was exceedingly shy, though she was a superb public speaker.*

1. He writes well, but he is no Shakespeare.

2. It just stands to reason that we need to balance our budget.

3. A budding genius, my little brother won a mathematics award and two science awards.

4. We could wait till hell freezes over to see a solution to hostilities in the Middle East.

5. The job of moving my grandfather to a nursing home was easier said than done.

6. I did not know for sure, but I had a sneaking suspicion that my friends were planning a surprise party.

7. Your message has come through loud and clear.

8. The sight of my old rival scared me out of my wits.

9. We may have to bite the bullet before we see an end to the budget crisis.

10. I nearly died when I saw the utility bill.

EXERCISE 31-7

Writing Concisely   *31c (p. 480)*

Revise the following paragraphs to eliminate empty words and phrases.

1   Interestingly enough, settlement of Manitoba began in the most inhospitable region of the province, with the exploration of the Hudson Bay area and the establishment of the Hudson Bay Company. Many explorers had been looking for the North-West Passage and stayed when fur trading posts were established in the remote and harsh area around Hudson Bay. The fur traders sent the pelts south, sometimes down the Red River, and then primarily through the Great Lakes system. The movement of the settlements then was also southward at first as the traders established these forts.

2   Agricultural settlement was next and it was begun around 1812 in the south and continued through adversity over the next 45 years. Conditions were very difficult. The settlers faced natural obstacles like hail, frost, floods, and grasshoppers. The farming settlers also faced non-agricultural obstacles like the struggle between the Hudson's Bay Company and the North West Company. The Hudson's Bay Company held a monopoly and

later took over the North West Company as well to keep the monopoly. The settlers also faced expansionism from people from the United States, and from Upper Canada wanting to take over their land. The settlers also experienced skirmishes with the Métis. In 1857 the British Government also sponsored an expedition to explore the fertile area northwest of the Red River Valley for settlement.

3   In 1870, the Hudson's Bay Company charter for the lands was terminated and the lands were taken over by the new Dominion of Canada and opened for further settlement. In 1881, the provincial boundaries were extended to form the present province. From 1876 to 1881, 40 000 immigrants, a great number of them British, from Ontario went west to take advantage of prime farmland. The British from Ontario were not the only immigrants to the new province. There were other settlers. The Mennonites, who settled primarily in the Steinbach and Winkler area, and the Icelandic settlers, who settled primarily near Gimli and Hecla, were other groups who came to the province.

4   The late 1890s and the early years of the twentieth century, from about 1897 to 1910, were years of great prosperity for the settlers who came then from all over the world. Some of the settlers came from Canada, the United Kingdom, the United States, and Eastern Europe. There were many different groups who came

to settle in Manitoba. The south experienced a booming agricul-turally based economy. Unfortunately, that boom was followed by a depression, first in 1913 and then a more serious depression in the 1930s.

5   Although the population in Manitoba has remained relatively stable, if there is a trend, it would be movement out of the province. However, the greatest irony is that there is a movement northward to some of the areas first settled. Since the end of World War II, the population has shifted northward, although that shift is relatively minor, because of the rapid growth of resource-based industry. Although the big industry is no longer the fur trade, the forbidding north is once again the attraction.

exer
31

Name _____ Date _____

Chapter 32 Using the Dictionary

EXERCISE 32-1

Using the Dictionary   *32a-b (pp. 489-497)*

Use a dictionary to answer the following questions.

Name of dictionary   _____

Date of publication   _____

A. Abbreviations and Symbols

Write out the meaning of the following abbreviations or symbols.

Example: n. pl. or pl. n. *plural noun*

a. *syn.* _____   d. *mil.* _____

b. *dial.* _____   e. *obs.* _____

c. *lit.* _____   f. *intr. v.* _____

B. Spelling

On the following lines, reproduce the way your dictionary lists the words given.

Example: dessertspoon *des.sert.spoon*

a. speakeasy _____   c. living room _____

b. backwater _____   d. catlike _____

e. hayloft _____   g. Italy _____

f. freeze-dry _____   h. self-government _____

C. Pronunciation

Copy out exactly the pronunciation given by your dictionary for the following words. If the dictionary gives more than one pronunciation for a word, provide both. Consulting the pronunciation key, sound out the word until you can pronounce it accurately and smoothly.

Example: beguile bi'gɪl

a. pastoral _____   e. often _____

b. err _____   f. Caribbean _____

c. invalid _____   g. kiln _____

d. schism _____   h. irrelevant _____

D. Grammatical Functions and Forms

1. List and label the past-tense and past-participle forms of the following verbs exactly as provided in your dictionary.

   Example: have *had (past tense and past participle)*

a. prefer _____

b. work _____

c. break _____

d. echo_____

e. wring _____

f. see _____

2. List and label the comparative and superlative forms of the following adjectives and adverbs exactly as given in your dictionary.

   Example: small *smaller (comparative), smallest (superlative)*

   beautiful *(no forms given)*

a. inner

b. lovely

c. cross *(adj.)*

d. ill

e. median

E. Etymology

1. Trace the origins of the words listed below as they are given in
   your dictionary. List (1) the initial language and word from which
   our word is derived; (2) the meaning of the initial word (sometimes not listed separately if it is the same as the given word); and
   (3) the other languages through which the word has passed on its
   way to us. Use the full names of languages, not abbreviations
   (consult the key to the dictionary's abbreviations if necessary).
   The guide to the dictionary will tell you how to read the etymology of a word if you need help.

   Example: logic (1) *Greek logos*

   (2) *speech, reason*

   (3) *Late Latin, Old French, Middle English*

a. induce (1)

   (2)

   (3)

b. lieutenant (1)

   (2)

   (3)

c. shirt   (1) _____

                 (2) _____

                 (3) _____

d. rhythm   (1) _____

                 (2) _____

                 (3) _____

2. Provide the origins of the following words as they are given in your dictionary.

     Example: ohm   *After Georg Simon Ohm (1787-1854),*

                         German physicist

a. zipper _____

b. jargon _____

c. astronaut _____

d. jerk _____

e. quisling ___   _____

F. Meanings

     List two different meanings for each of the following words as they appear in your dictionary.

a. specie *(n.)* (1) _____

                 (2) _____

b. gall *(n.)*   (1) _____

                 (2) _____

c. hound *(v.)* (1) _____

                 (2) _____

d. go *(v.)*   (1) _____

                 (2) _____

G. Labels

Provide the label applied by your dictionary to each of the following words or meanings of words.

Example: ain't *nonstandard (not appropriate for standard written English)*

a. critter (noun meaning "animal") _____

_____

b. enthuse (verb meaning "to show enthusiasm") _____

_____

c. knock (verb meaning "to criticize") _____

_____

H. Other Information

1 Where does your dictionary provide biographical information on important persons: in the main alphabetical listing or in a separate section? (Give the page numbers if a separate section.)

_____

2. Where does your dictionary provide geographical information on countries, cities, rivers, mountains, and so on: in the main alphabetical listing or in a separate section? (Give the page numbers if a separate section.)

_____

3. Does your dictionary contain a history of the English language?

   _____

4. Does your dictionary contain a guide to punctuation and mechanics?

   _____

5. Does your dictionary contain a list of colleges and universities?

   _____

Name _____ Date _____

Chapter 33 Improving Your Vocabulary

EXERCISE 33-1

Using Roots, Prefixes, and Suffixes   *33a-b (pp. 498-505)*

By referring to the lists of roots, prefixes, and suffixes given on pages 480-483, identify each word below as a noun *(n.)*, verb *(v.)*, or adjective *(adj.)* and guess at its meaning. If you are unable to guess, look the word up in your dictionary.

   Example: antebellum *before a war (adj.)*

1. belligerent _____

2. anterior _____

3. prorate _____

4. retroactive _____

5. advocate _____

6. Francophile _____

exer
33

7. interdict _____

8. polymer _____

9. subvert _____

10. transceiver _____

266

11. kilocycle _____

12. intersperse _____

13. demagogue _____

14. amoral _____

15. transcend _____

EXERCISE 33-2

Learning New Words Through Context   *33c (p. 505)*

Use contextual clues to guess at the meanings of the italicized words in the passages below. Write out the meanings. Then check your definitions in your dictionary.

1. His sole aim in *augmenting* his income was to buy a swimming pool, a luxury car, and other trappings of *hedonism.*

   augment_____

   hedonism _____

2. The newspaper's *spurious* argument was based on forged statistics and a *paucity* of real evidence.

   spurious _____

   paucity _____

3. A *genealogist* may spend hours looking through birth records, baptismal certificates, marriage licences, death warrants, and ship passenger lists and still not find any *substantive* information on your family.

   genealogist_____

   substantive _____

4. His *gaffe* of calling the teacher by the wrong name went unnoticed, for the teacher was *immersed* in a calculus problem.

   gaffe _____

   immersed_____

5. Sue seemed to be *ubiquitous*. When I went to the post office, she was there. When I went to the bank, she was there. When I came home, she was in front of the house, walking her dog.

ubiquitous _____

Chapter 34 Spelling

EXERCISE 34-1

Practising Spelling Rules   *34a-c (pp. 508-521)*

A. Insert *ie* or *ei* in the following blanks.

1. ach _____ ve   8. n _____ ther

2. w _____ ght   9. bel _____ ve

3. fr _____ nd   10. hyg _____ ne

4. ch _____ f   11. forf _____ t

5. sl _____ gh   12. conc _____ t

6. h _____ ght   13. s _____ ze

7. rec _____ ve   14. dec _____ t

B. Keep or drop the final *e* or *y* as necessary when adding endings to the following words. Consult your dictionary as necessary.

Example: supply + -er *supplier* _____

1. notice + -ing _____

   notice + -able _____

2. hate + -ing _____

   hate + -ful _____

3. sure + -ly _____

   sure + -est _____

4. agree + -ing _____

   agree + -able _____

5. duty + -ful _____

   duly + -s _____

6. true + -est _____

   true + -ly _____

7. defy + -ing _____

   defy + -ance _____

8. study + -ing _____

   study + -ed _____

C. Write the correct forms for these words.

   Example: hop + ing *hopping*

1. differ + ence _____   7. begin + ing _____

2. travel + ed _____   8. stop + ing _____

3. submit + ed _____   9. prefer + ence _____

4. refer + ed _____   10. prefer + ing _____

5. occur + ence _____   11. ship + ment _____

6. permit + ed _____   12. beg + ing _____

D. Write the plurals of the following words and compounds, checking your dictionary as needed.

Example: chief   *chiefs* _____

1. buffalo _____
2. tomato _____
3. mother-in-law _____
4. sheep _____
5. shelf _____
6. fox _____
7. series _____

8. index _____
9. bureau _____
10. handful _____
11. passerby _____
12. analysis _____
13. economy _____
14. ox _____

EXERCISE 34-2

Using the Hyphen in Compound Words, Fractions, and Compound Numbers   *34d (p. 521)*

A. Write out the following numbers, using hyphens when appropriate.

> *Example:* 4500   *forty-five hundred* _____

1. 10 1/4 _____

2. 21/22_____

3. 39 _____

4. 102 _____

5. 3 000 152 _____

6. 92 _____

7. 25 _____

8. 25 095_____

9. 3/10_____

10. 260 _____

B. As appropriate for correct spelling, leave each of the following groups of words as they are, insert a hyphen, or close up the space. Check your dictionary as needed.

> *Example:* anti Soviet   *anti-Soviet* _____

1. ante bellum _____

exer
34

2. pro Canadian _____

3. self serving _____

4. car port _____

5. porch light _____

6. news stand _____

7. hot dog _____

8. non partisan _____

9. ninth century warfare _____

10. co author _____

11. post Victorian _____

12. red eyed rabbit _____

13. re shuffle _____

14. long handled _____

15. red handed _____

16. soft hearted _____

17. pre fabricated _____

18. life boat _____

19. life like _____

20. anti imperialist _____

Part VIII RESEARCH WRITING

Chapters 35-39

EXERCISE 36-1

Writing Paraphrases   36b (p. 572)

Write paraphrases of the following passages. Remember that paraphrases are often as long as the original. They do not use the phrasing of the original.

> *Example:* "The web of life in the oceans, perhaps more than any other part of the environment, is vulnerable to damage from increased ultraviolet radiation."—Jonathan Schell, *The Fate of the Earth* (New York: Knopf, 1982), 86.
>
> *In The Fate of the Earth, Jonathan Schell tells us that ocean life is particularly susceptible to harm from ultraviolet radiation (86).*

1. "Galileo had believed Copernican theory (that the planets orbited the sun) since early on, but it was only when he found the evidence needed to support the idea that he started to publicly support it."—Stephen W. Hawking, *A Brief History of Time: From the Big Bang to Black Holes* (New York: Bantam, 1988), 179.

exer
36

2. "In April of 1919, in Paris, the President of the United States suffered, according to all evidence available after the fact, a throm-
bosis in his brain. His illness was diagnosed as influenza by his
doctor—a logical diagnosis at a time when influenza outbreaks
were sweeping the world."—Gene Smith, *When the Cheering
Stopped: The Last Years of Woodrow Wilson* (New York: Time,
1964), 101.

3. "It is certainly foolish to learn nothing from experience, but we
can learn too much from it. Indeed, one way of defining a bureau-
cracy might be that it is an organization that has learned so much
from the past that it can't learn anything from the present."—
John Holt, *Freedom and Beyond* (New York: Dell, 1972), 45.

4. "Knowledge of human nature is the beginning and end of political education, but several years of arduous study in the neighborhood of Westminster led Henry Adams to think that knowledge of English human nature had little or no value outside of England. In Paris, such a habit stood in one's way; in America it roused all the instincts of native jealousy."—Henry Adams, *The Education of Henry Adams: An Autobiography,* Vol. I (New York: Time, 1964), 198.

5. "The law is constantly expanding and changing: it does not initiate social change, but does respond—slowly—to demands and pressures from the people it is supposed to serve. It follows the public consciousness into various levels of awareness about society and its institutions. It legitimizes or 'guarantees' specific rights only after those rights have been won on another battlefield."—Jean Strouse, *Up Against the Law: The Legal Rights of People Under Twenty-One* (New York: Signet, 1970), 20.

exer
36

Name _____ Date _____

EXERCISE 36-2

Avoiding Plagiarism   *36c (p. 581)*

Examine the following paired passages to see if the paraphrase plagia-
rizes the original. Underline plagiarized words and rewrite the passages to eliminate the plagiarism. If there is no plagiarism, write OK
in the space below the paraphrases.

> *Example:* "The opportunity given to the Romans by their language
> was made the more compelling and inviting by the
> nature of Roman education. For all its faults, the pro-
> nouncedly linguistic and literary bent of the system
> seemed specially calculated to produce orators and writ-
> ers."—Michael Grant, *The World of Rome* (New York:
> New American Library, 1960), 235.
>
> Michael Grant claims that the Roman language and edu-
> cation seemed <u>specially calculated for producing orators
> and writers</u> (235).
>
> *Michael Grant claims that a special effect of the
> Roman language and education was the produc-
> tion of orators and writers (235).*

1. "For centuries of ever-growing exaltation—the centuries when
   the Roman empire was at its zenith—the passionate Mystery religions supplied these wants, and also provided the cohesion, the
   community spirit, which was not available in so encouraging a
   form from any other source."—Michael Grant, *The World of
   Rome* (New York: New American Library, 1960), 185.

   When the Roman empire was at its zenith, the passionate Mystery
   religions provided community spirit (Grant 185).

2. "Unlike the teaching of the Epicureans, the Stoic injunction *live consistently with nature* was meant ethically. Conscience and duty were the keynotes of Stoic ethics, and the prime duty of the soul was to realize its moral perfectability."—Michael Grant, *The World of Rome* (New York: New American Library, 1960), 218.

   Stoics were concerned mainly with ethics and moral perfectability.

3. "On August 21 General de Castelnau heard that his son had been killed in the battle. To his staff who tried to express their sympathy, he said after a moment's silence, in a phrase that was to become something of a slogan for France, 'We will continue, gentlemen.'"—Barbara Tuchman, *The Guns of August* (New York, Dell: 1962), 264.

   The World War I slogan "We will continue, gentlemen," has been attributed to General de Castelnau, expressed to his staff on the death of his son (Tuchman 264).

4. "There is no record what Asquith replied or what, in his almost mind, a region difficult to penetrate under the best of circumstances, he thought on this crucial question."—Barbara Tuchman, *The Guns of August* (New York, Dell: 1962), 72.

   We don't know what Asquith's almost mind thought about this question (72).

5. "The records of palaeontology provide evidence of the changing shapes of continents and the changing flow of the ocean currents, for these earlier earth patterns account for the otherwise mysterious present distribution of many plants and animals."—Rachel Carson, *The Edge of the Sea* (New York: New American Library, 1955), 30.

The mysterious distribution of animals and plants is accounted for by changing continent shapes and changing flow of ocean currents.